WAL

— THE —
TORS & HILLTOPS
OF DARTMOOR

A. D. JOHNSON

Peninsula
Press

First published in 2002 by Peninsula Press,
an imprint of Forest Publishing
Woodstock
Liverton
Newton Abbot
Devon TQ12 6JJ

Copyright © A. D. Johnson 2002

British Library Cataloguing in Publication Data

A catalogue record for this book is available from the British Library.

ISBN 1-872640-49-4

Editorial, design and layout by:
Mike Lang

Front cover illustration by:
John W. Taylor

Typeset by:
Carnaby Typesetting, Torquay, Devon TQ1 1EG

Printed and bound in Great Britain by:
Cromwell Press Ltd, Trowbridge, Wiltshire BA14 0XB

Contents

Introduction

Dartmoor enjoys a reputation for isolation and wildness, which is founded on images of the bleak prospect of Dartmoor Prison and the fiction of Conan Doyle. Visitors to Devon will understand this reputation when they look at the hills above Okehampton from the A30, or when they stare into the depths of the southern moor from the roads to Princetown. In fact the moor, as it is known locally, is quite small and is close to the cities of Exeter and Plymouth. From Tavistock in the west to Moretonhampstead in the east can take little more than 40 minutes by car, and few of the hilltops rise higher than 600 metres.

For the experienced British hillwalker the moor's reputation may, therefore, seem overstated when compared, for example, with Snowdonia or the Fells, where heights and distances are much greater. But the moor is a tough place for the Ten Tors teams criss-crossing its empty hills and valleys in the spring and early summer, and also for the young Duke of Edinburgh Award expedition teams which explore its depths on foot throughout the year. The ground can be steep and marshy, perspectives can be confusing and the weather can be chancy. Dartmoor is, therefore, a national park to be treated with respect and care: mistakes in navigation can be penalised, at the very least by wet feet, but at worst by hypothermia. But it should also be treated with respect and care because of its beauty: it is at its best in the early morning or at dusk, and also during those months which mark the unfolding from spring into summer and then from summer into autumn. At such times these English uplands are a visual feast of light and shadow, of misty panoramas and green secrets.

Lists of peaks are published for many of the upland areas of Britain, and Dartmoor is no exception. William Crossing published an appendix of tors in his *A Hundred Years on Dartmoor* (1901), and other lists appear in *A Pocket Guide to the Tors and Hills of Dartmoor* (1994) by A. Stevens, in R. E. Downard's *The Tors of Dartmoor* (1982), and in T. Bound's *The A to Z of Dartmoor Tors* (1991). The national park is a very busy tourist destination which attracts visitors throughout the year from overseas and from all over the country, and whether visitors picnic alongside their cars or seek isolation on foot a handy checklist of the tors and hilltops is both informative and a record. Indeed, it is for this reason that I have included an up-to-date and accessible list of all peaks within the bounds of Dartmoor which have the title 'tor' on the Landranger Ordnance Survey Map 1:25,000, or are significant hilltops. This, combined with a collection of 20 different walks to separate tors and hilltops, grouped together by the four seasons in order to portray the panorama of a Dartmoor year, will, hopefully, provide the reader with some 'colour' – either in anticipation of delights yet to come, or in recollection of past Dartmoor pleasures. Happy walking!

The Tors

For visitors to Devon a tor should be a distinctive rocky crag, ringed by concentric contour lines on the map, and rising high on the skyline. However, the compiler of a comprehensive list is always challenged by the question of what to include and what to exclude, and Dartmoor poses its own problems. For instance, not every tor is on Dartmoor – Brent Tor, with its tiny church, is the most distinctive tor of all but it lies close to a village and is separated from the open moor by some miles of agricultural land. Not every peak bears the name of 'tor' – the highest top is High Willhays at 621 metres. Some small rocky outcrops have local names not on the principal maps, whilst other tors are little more than frost-shattered remnants or have been quarried almost out of existence. For the compiler the more rugged northern moor, where heights reach 600m, poses fewer problems than the south, where, despite being cut by rivers and steep-sided valleys, the ground is generally less harsh and there are few real peaks and not so many named tors.

The etymology of the word 'tor' has been inconclusively explored by the compilers of dictionaries: it is clearly very old, and appears to share the same phonetic base as the word 'tower'. Its widespread use in this small area is, however, unique, with only a few examples occurring elsewhere in Britain or continental Europe.

The National Park

The Dartmoor National Park Authority has its offices at Bovey Tracey and provides information and guidance for visitors in well-prepared bureaux at various tourist centres on and around the moor: the most significant of these is the High Moorland Visitor Centre at Princetown.

Visitors should use designated parking areas. Most areas are readily accessible, but those which are not are clearly marked on the better maps. Please do not clamber over stone walls or through fences, and do use the stiles or walk alongside obstructions until a true footpath is evident. Please look after this wonderful amenity so that it is conserved for use by future generations.

Safety

The moor is an area to be treated with respect. Without taking a few sensible precautions visitors may suffer personal injury or loss of property. The following notes are offered as guidance:–

Climate and clothing: Long-distance walkers on the moor should be prepared for upland north European conditions, with the possibility of precipitation and wind. Windproofs, waterproofs, insulation and good boots are essential.

Navigation: Rapid changes in visibility, accompanied by wind and rain or mist, are usual. Walkers should carry good quality maps and compasses, and use them. Few areas of the moor are very far from a road, and it is possible to 'walk out' of most situations.

Injuries: The Dartmoor Rescue Group provides Mountain Rescue facilities. Walking parties which suffer casualties should contact the emergency services giving their six-figure grid reference.

Military Ranges: Areas of the northern moor are used for live firing. Visual warnings are given by flags and lamps (at night), but, in order to avoid a wasted journey on the northern moor, walkers are advised to check with local post offices or libraries before setting out, or to telephone Freephone 0800 458 4868.

Theft: Endeavour to park close to other vehicles, do not leave anything of importance in the car and please report anything suspicious. Be prepared for vandalism. Dartmoor is close to large conurbations and visitors' cars lure thieves to even the busiest car parks.

A. D. Johnson

March 2002

Spring

1. Cox Tor, Roos Tor & Great/Middle Staple Tors

2. Brat Tor, Great Links Tor & Arms Tor

3. Leather Tor, Sharpitor & Peek Hill

4. Sharp Tor, Luckey Tor, Yar Tor & Corndon Down

Great Staple Tor

G Thurlow

1. Cox Tor, Roos Tor & Great/Middle Staple Tors

Start and finish: SX 531752
Distance: 4.5km (2³/4 miles)
Approximate time: 2 hours

'Honeypot' is the tourist management term for sites which exert a strong pull on visitors. The car park on the crest of the hill overlooking Tavistock from the Tavistock to Princetown road is such a honeypot. On a bank holiday it is complete with ice cream van, brightly-coloured kites fluttering in the breeze and the constant coming and going of cars with number plates from all over Great Britain and Europe. The hill on which it is sited is called Pork Hill, a steep 150m gain in height up the road from its base to a viewing point in the bottom corner of the car park. The park is overlooked from the north by Cox Tor, a further 120m higher and with an even better view – which you will shortly enjoy!

These steep western slopes of Dartmoor are the first significant hills to meet the south-westerly wind from the empty Atlantic Ocean. The rushing air is forced upwards and transformed, sometimes into high white cloud, sometimes into low clinging mist and sometimes into rain. And when the weather is right these steep slopes and the surging air also attract the hang-gliders.

Park your car here (remembering to lock it securely and to remove any valuables), cross the road ahead and step out directly for the top of Cox Tor, due north. The path is broad, inviting, green, little worn and springy underfoot. To your left is a wide vista into Cornwall, to your right the panorama of tors north of Merrivale. The ascent is gentle at first, but higher up it gradually tightens until you reach two abrupt 'steps', where the strollers separate from the walkers and head back to their cars. The moor affords equal pleasure to all its visitors, whether they linger beside the open door of their vehicle, or tread gingerly across the inviting heath in trainers more accustomed to tarmac pavements than wet peat, but it is surprising how empty the inner fastness of the moor remains on even the busiest holiday. There is an exception: during May inner Dartmoor crawls with teams of young men and women preparing for the annual Ten Tors challenge, and at every summit you will meet a group studying their maps and eating their Kendal Mint Cake. They will return in years to come to enjoy this national park at their leisure, and also leave their cars behind!

Pause on top of the first short rise, alongside a little quarry to your right, and look back to the busy road and car park, then beyond to Tavistock nestling in its river valley and, finally, out to Plymouth Sound and the English Channel,

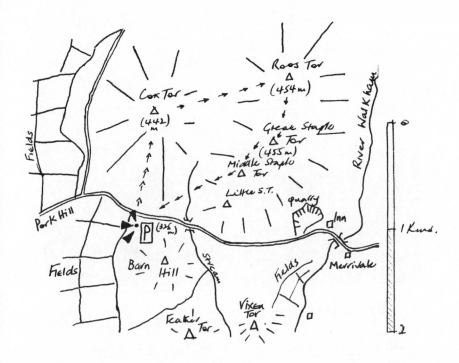

gleaming silver on the farthest horizon. On the path below you there will be parties walking up and down; on the path above there will be one or two groups climbing to, and descending from, the summit. Walk on, over the second step, and then head for the rocks ahead of you – the fore summit of the tor – from where the view has opened up a little more so that you can see the Tamar Bridges and Brent Tor. The true top of the tor is marked by the trig point and tumble of dark grey granite rocks at 442m, about 150m of level walking from the fore summit. The western slope of the tor is steep and covered in clitter, rough and difficult going.

Turn your back on the westerly views and look into the moor: at the jewel green fields of the little Wedlake Valley just below, starkly contrasted with the faded moorland colours around. The mountain village of Peter Tavy is out of sight, cut-off by folds in the land, but its sister, Mary Tavy, is clearly visible, and opposite you, across the wide shallow valley to the east, are Roos Tor and Great Staple Tor. There is a little settlement of prehistoric hut circles stonily scattered on the slope and best seen in the long shadows of early sunlight. Beyond is Great Mis Tor and, to its right, the telecommunications mast on North Hessary Tor. From here, with the air soughing across the heather, bringing the smell of moist upland air and the scent of peat, the world seems limitless and the silence palpable. A few cattle

Cox Tor, looking towards Roos Tor (left) and Great Staple Tor.

Karen Lang

move slowly in the empty valley, and the glittering surface of the small seasonal pool is ruffled by the wind, scattering the blue reflection of a bright sky.

Leave the trig point, heading for the pool and Roos Tor beyond. Underfoot the dried marshland has left a strange formation of tiny drumlins, but the descent is easy. The pool dries out in hot summers but all water improves a landscape, this tiny fragment of 'glass' no less than the lake at Burrator. Roos Tor has a large mushroom-capped rock, and the slopes are patterned by swirls of clitter fixed for all time as the snows and rock-shattering frosts of the last Ice Age deposited them. It is a monumental pile of granite: the dark grey rocks here marked by white laths of feldspar – the crystal structures embedded in the stone – and occasionally discoloured by the pink or red of other minerals. The tor is topped by a mast, which carries a large red flag when firing exercises are taking place, for this is part of the army training area. Below is the valley of the River Walkham.

Great Staple Tor is perhaps the most distinctive summit on the moor. Its tall 6m granite stacks (steeples?), separated by a broad avenue of close-cropped turf, are visible from miles around. Head for them across the wide and shallow bowl of pale grass. If the wind is from the north study the clouds ahead of you in the southern sky: small white clouds looking for all the world like inverted saucers are called lenticular clouds. They form in the lee of high ground, where ripples of moist air stream upwards into colder temperatures to appear briefly as cloud vapour before descending again and becoming invisible. With a north wind, such clouds sometimes form to the south of the moor, especially in late spring when the air is still cold enough to support them.

The avenue between the two towers of granite is a familiar feature of Dartmoor's tors. The larger rock formations are often split by such flat expanses of rock-free ground, and you can explore similar geological effects at Hound Tor, Ingra Tor and elsewhere. The top of the western tower is difficult of access, but the eastern tower can be topped out with a bit of ungymnastic effort and a helpful shove from below. Worth the effort!

The two towers of granite on Great Staple Tor.

Author

From here you drop down to Middle Staple Tor. Below you is Merrivale Quarry which survived to provide building granite until very recently, and on the gentler slopes above Merrivale, on the other side of the Walkham, is the best group of ancient stones on this side of the moor: two parallel double stone rows, hut circles, kistvaens and obelisks. From Middle Staple Tor you can see your car again, no doubt surrounded by a horde of others. The descent is straightforward and takes you through the narrow ravine of an abandoned tin working and across a couple of shallow streams before reaching the road adjacent to the car park.

This is a tourist route because of the easy public access to Cox Tor's remarkable views. Lend it some spice by getting on top of one of Great Staple Tor's unique columns of granite.

——2. Brat Tor, Great Links Tor & Arms Tor——

Start and finish: SX 525853
Distance: 7–8km (4¹/₄ – 5 miles)
Approximate time: 2 – 2¹/₂ hours

Dartmoor's granite bulk rises from the lowlands of southern England, in dark and naked contrast to the green and verdant countryside of Devon. The difference is stark in the north, where the highest ground looms above the A30 and the hills show their sunless slopes to travellers. From the Sourton road south to Tavistock, which cuts a clean line between the heathland to the east and the farms and villages to the west, Dartmoor's western aspect is more welcoming. Light floods the golden slopes and comfortable inns stand at successive road junctions, beside signposts to nearby villages. This walk starts near Lydford, a remarkable survival of a Saxon settlement and worth a separate visit. In its time more important than Exeter, and the wealthy target of Viking raids, its looted treasures have been found in buried hoards in Scandinavia, and its Saxon street plan survives intact. The square castle was, in fact, a prison: the real castle is a green motte and bailey standing in an excellent defensive position behind the church.

Opposite the turn to Lydford from the Tavistock road, by the Dartmoor Inn, is a track which will take a saloon car, heading east through a wooden gate, to parking on the common land beyond. On a late spring day, when the trees are still bare and the rhododendron's cascade of purple flowers tumbles across the surrounding garden walls, the north-west wind can bite through the heat of the sun and you will find that you need windproofs!

From the car park the sward rises gently to a nearby crest, and the moor's peaks stand guard on the horizon beyond. Overhead the sky is scraped blue bone clean by the wind, but the growing heat of the sun has sketched in a few high brilliant white clouds. As your path brings you to the top of the heath pause, and compare your map with the panorama on the other side of the valley. On your left is the swelling mound of Great Nodden, then the peak of Arms Tor which you will visit later on, and, just beyond, peeping over the horizon, is the top of Great Links Tor, your objective for the day. Straight ahead is Brat Tor with distinctive Widgery Cross, where you will be standing in half an hour, and then, to the right, are Doe Tor, Hare Tor and Ger Tor.

Walk downhill over the swelling downland into the valley of the River Lyd, towards the water. To your right, the course of the stream takes it through a small gorge, a lovely picnic spot for families, and worth a visit to read the memorial to a young subaltern killed in 1918: *"dulce et decorum est..."*. Your route, however, is towards the wooden bridge beside the gorse-covered

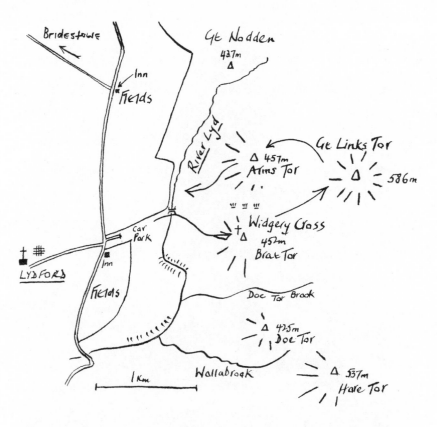

drystone wall, for use when the river is in spate. The stepping stones are more pleasant!

From the other side strike out for Widgery Cross, erected in 1887 to celebrate Queen Victoria's Golden Jubilee. It is self-evidently a steep ascent, almost 140m in height from ford to cross, with a choice of routes through the heather, gorse and rocks. Go straight up. Initially it is easy going, and you will flush out an occasional skylark, loudly musical in its agitation and deceit. Gradually the path steepens, calling for more effort, and ahead and above the cross on the summit disappears from sight beyond the looming first horizon. Towards the top, ahead and a little to your right, is a distinctive granite dyke, sloping downwards. Reach the foot of the dyke and then scramble up to the left, following the rocks. If you are lucky, in a sheltered spot you may see a lizard scampering for cover. Suddenly the cross reappears, close ahead, on top of Brat Tor, and 2km distant on your left is Great Links Tor. Scramble up to the top of the tor through a cleft in the rock and shelter from the wind alongside the granite cross in a position where you can also absorb some

Widgery Cross.
Karen Lang

warmth from the spring sun. The view from here is to the west, across a soft pastoral landscape of forests, fields and villages, and fading into a near blue haze which seems more blown in by the wind than blown away. Inland is the heart of the northern moor.

Descend on the moorland side of Widgery Cross and head for Great Links Tor. Although it appears to be level going, there is actually another 130m of ascent ahead. The turf is springy underfoot and unfolds gently north-east towards Great Links' peak of 586m. To your left, and level with Widgery Cross, is Arms Tor. Away to the right the swelling curves of the southern tors break like crests of frozen waves pounding the shore of Devon. Another lark ascends. The path is very easy after the stiff pull up to Widgery Cross.

Great Links Tor is initially unimpressive. The trig point stands on a separate pinnacle to the left, slightly lower than the summit, and the tor itself looks like a heap of plates stacked for washing up. Closer to, the solid granite bulk looms impressively over the flat surrounding turf, and it becomes apparent that there is no easy way to the top. If you really want to get up (and it is worth the effort) shimmy up one of the two little 'chimneys' on the southern side, *but not if there are crows' nests there.*

Whether from on top, or from the north-east side of the rock, the view across the drop into the valley under the tor and into the moor is immense. Stately cloud shadows move slowly across the vast and empty golden heath, and, farther on, the distant lower land is quilted by a patchwork of green fields. Widgery Cross and Arms Tor seem insignificant and low-lying.

Beyond, and to the east, are the remains of the peat industry: thousands of tons of peat were removed from here until it ended in the mid-50s. The 1950s! Peat then was used for fuel. Only today's moneyed leisure allows its import and misuse as a garden restorative.

The summit rocks of Great Links Tor.
Karen Lang

The route heads back to Arms Tor, dropping 130m directly down. The tor seems scattered from above, with the silhouette of the closest rocks black against the afternoon sky beyond. Keep to the higher ground: the valley to the left between Arms Tor and Brat Tor can be wet. Pick your way to the top of the rocks and enjoy the view from these outlying outcrops, breasting out over the western world. Finally descend due west, going straight down to the base of the hill where you should stop and look back. From here Arms Tor is an impressive bastion, 130m above.

Head back in the sunshine to the car. It should have taken you about two hours, perhaps two and a half. Time for tea in Lydford.

3. Leather Tor, Sharpitor & Peek Hill

Start and finish: SX 568693
Distance: 5km (3 miles)
Approximate time: 1¹/₂ hours

Leather Tor, viewed from the south.

Author

An expanse of water brings harmony to a landscape. Stretched blue and calm under its surrounding hills and embraced by a forested shoreline, Burrator is the most attractive of Dartmoor's lakes. They are all artificial. Fernworthy, Venford, Meldon and Avon Dam are reservoirs, too, and each has its charm, but none is so large or as well situated. In addition, the eastern end of the lake provides a good starting point for walks into the moor south of Princetown.

The lake's level and narrow perimeter road is used by runners, cyclists and walkers, and on the narrow beach there is an occasional fisherman. South West Water owns the surrounding catchment, maintaining the environment assiduously by including an arboretum suitable for wheelchairs as well as for toddlers, and signposted routes through the surrounding woods for the more agile. Norsworthy Bridge, where this short and stimulating walk starts, is popular, and there will be visitors parked off the road at almost any time.

The two crags reflected in this calm mirror are Sheeps Tor to the south, a broad-shouldered sentinel above the village of Sheepstor, and Leather Tor to

the north. Glimpsed in profile through the overhanging trees at Norsworthy
Bridge, Leather Tor's bare grey rocks rise above the surrounding grass and
heather to loom in an almost alpine style above the dark green stands of pine.
Seen from here, Leather Tor presents a steep and rugged walk, but with the
promise of excellent views out over the lake.

Your route takes you anti-clockwise round the lake, crossing the stream with
its surrounding carpets of irises, with the lake out of sight behind the trees on
your left. Immediately after crossing Norsworthy Bridge turn right and, with
the tip of Leather Tor directly ahead, cross over the stile; then follow the
footpath steeply upwards. In the late spring you will wade through a flame
yellow sea of gorse edged, on your right, by beech woods touched with the
first soft haze of leaf. Under the heat of the late morning sun the scents of pine
and herbs are drawn out and fill the air. Underfoot, the sunlight spins jewels
from dew on spiders' webs, and the only sound is birdsong from the beech
trees. The path winds on through the bushes upwards towards another stile and

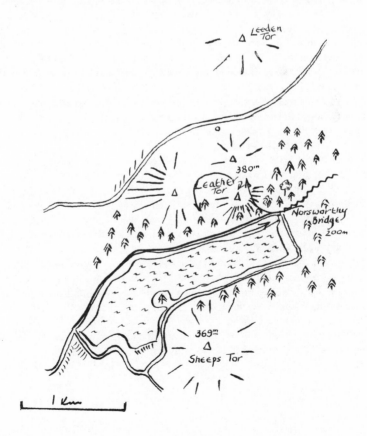

beyond to the distant, darker green of pine trees. Ignore the signposts beside the track, cross over and step up beside the Devonport Leat flowing from right to left. Some of the leat water flows into the reservoir. Built in the late 18th century, it was engineered to follow the contours drawing fresh water to the coast and the busy town of Devonport, now part of Plymouth. Follow it right, to the little stone bridge formed from granite gateposts, and then cross the water to stand on the heather and grass at the foot of Leather Tor. From here the route is hard work. A steady upward plod past dwarf oak, with violets and cuckoo flowers underfoot, and threading through the jumbled maze of boulders, rocks and clitter. To your right the line of forestry pine trees enfolds its dark and grassless shadows, and to your left a harsh ridge of granite tumbles down the slope towards the leat and the trees. It is hard and steep going (a proper climb), and it can be warm work. Behind you, the lake, Down Tor and Sheeps Tor are rising into view.

Look ahead at the tor, which is actually much closer than it looks! On Dartmoor everything is on a modest scale and even an 'alpine' route takes only a few minutes. Your objective is the deep notch at the left-hand end of the peak. Make your way steadily up towards it, using your hands if necessary to heave up and over some of the larger rocks as the ground gets steeper, but really it is almost possible to stay on turf all the way to a point just below the top. When you reach the cleft you must have some sense of achievement – you have ascended 150m in a very short distance, and the ground falls steeply away below your boots. But do not stop here. Scramble up the right-hand side of the notch to reach the crest of Leather Tor in order to enjoy the walk along the lofty ridge, and of course, the view. These things are why you are here, on this the best little scramble on the moor, looking out across the green woods and the blue water of Burrator.

Even on the brightest of days the weather can change quickly, so do not be surprised if, after a warm ascent with the sun on your back, you are confronted from the top by massed squadrons of grey clouds scudding in from the west and north-west, seemingly at eye level, and sweeping across the darkening landscape of the moor. Against this backdrop is Sharpitor, a little higher at almost 400m and the same distance from the northern foot of Leather Tor. It is an easy walk across the almost level turf and a simple scramble to the top, with the Princetown road beneath you, the small pool by the road a broken fragment of mirror tumbled from heaven. There is a view, and a good one, out towards the old railway line and Leeden Tor. There is another from Peek Hill, an easy walk 500m to the south-west. But all of this is really secondary to the pleasure of ascending Leather Tor from Norsworthy Bridge.

Descend steeply from Peek Hill towards the lake, cross the leat again and then pick up the road back to Norsworthy Bridge.

4. Sharp Tor, Luckey Tor, Yar Tor & Corndon Down

Start and finish: SX 685735
Distance: 6km (3³/4 miles)
Approximate time: 3 hours

Dartmoor is the source for most of Devon's large rivers, and where their upper watercourses cut out of the moorland the twisting valleys, steep granite slopes and high tors fuse into dramatic landscapes. Tavy Cleave in the west, the Dart Valley in the centre, the Avon in the south and the Teign in the north. There are others besides. Each one is striking but distinctive, and each has its proponents, but surely the most beautiful is the Dart?

This walk takes in part of the Dart Valley, just below the confluence of the West and East Dart at Dartmeet. It takes you down some long steep drops and back up equally sustained ascents, but it goes on to easy level downland walking and ends with a crown of massive cairns looking into the centre of the moor. There are some impressive contrasts in the scenery, and also between moments of solitude near the river and the busy tourist traffic on the road to Dartmeet.

Park off the byroad to Sherwell, from where you can see the impressive little peak of the well-named Sharp Tor. It is your first destination. Walk down to

The western side of Sharp Tor.
Karen Lang

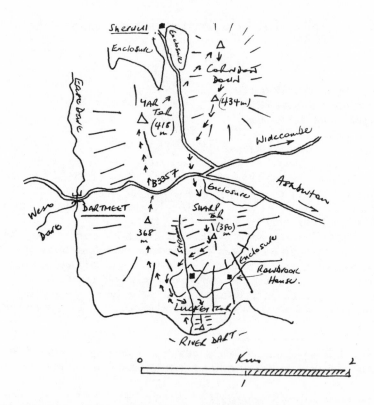

the main road and then stroll easily across the turf to the nearer of the two compact granite groups which make up the peak. Scramble to the top, then cross over to the next block and ascend that in its turn to the true summit at 380m.

Your reward is instant (and for very little effort!) with a tremendous view to your left, down the deep and twisting valley. Woodland pours down the steep slopes in a froth of foliage which spills out in places onto the upland above. On the other side of the river, directly opposite Sharp Tor, the smooth surface of Venford Reservoir gleams silver against the darkness of surrounding pine trees. But the source of all this beauty is invisible and silent. Beneath a canopy of leaves, and at the bottom of the valley, the glitter of light on the surface of the Dart and the roar of the water tumbling through its rocks are both lost, 200m below. You are high enough for a military helicopter on a low-level navigation exercise to occasionally appear *below* a visitor perched on this crag!

It is a steep descent from here, south-west, crossing the little stream at the bottom of the valley on your right. From there follow the narrow path uphill on the far side, keeping the fields of Rowbrook and their enclosing drystone wall on your left. Follow the wall round until it drops downhill and then turn back to the east. Pick your way following a rocky sheep track through patchy gorse until you are confronted by the little valley of the same stream, now dropping steeply to the Dart. Move away from the wall, into the heather, going carefully downhill until you pick up another narrow path heading left, upstream into trees. Under the tangle of their low dark branches is a crossing; muddy and stony, with the path continuing on the other side. Before proceeding under the trees look across this tiny valley to pick out the rocks of Luckey Tor, half-hidden by low trees, on the other side. Luckey Tor is your next stop.

Follow the narrow path on the other side, through trees, until you reach pasture and a wider track. Navigation is tricky: note the details for your return!

A wide and easy path then takes you quickly down to the tor. The approach is bowered by fragrant hawthorn with abundant white blossom in late May, blushed with strokes of faint pink, and with a carpet of bluebells spread between the trees. The top of the tor is close by, modestly lost in a tangle of dwarf trees. Scramble along the top, dodging low birch branches: even before you reach the far end the roar of the water rises to meet you. Peer over the big drop, surrounded by trees. You may see a couple of helmeted rock climbers, but below them is a snooker-table-smooth grassy floor – the valley bottom. The river is still out of sight, screened by leaves and branches, but you can descend further if you wish (and it is worth the trip). It is, however, steep, dirty and hard work coming back up.

Now for the way back: an ascent of 168m to Yartor Down. Drop down from the rocks to the grass alongside and retrace your steps to the stream, thence back to the drystone wall surrounding Rowbrook Farm. Use every opportunity to gain height: it is good exercise and there are enough sheep trails to keep you out of the bracken most of the time! Beyond the wall push on to the highest point above, until you reach the broad featureless crest of Yartor Down, an expanse of dense gorse with a wide path at its heart leading back to the main road. Cross over and head up, more gently now, to Yar Tor, having recovered all the height lost since leaving Sharp Tor an hour and a half earlier.

Yar Tor is another contrast, with a curious cairn and overlooking the bustling tourist car park, restaurant and shop at Dartmeet, 170m below. Where Sharp Tor is compact, Yar Tor is an unassembled jigsaw of huge granite blocks. Yar Tor is also littered with prehistoric remains: a stone row, hut circles, field system and tumulus. Whereas Sharp Tor looks south into the wooded Dart Valley, Yar Tor looks north and west over the East Dart towards moorland and tors. On the northern edge of the tor is a large pulpit-shaped rock: climb to the top and stand for a few minutes on top of the moorland world.

Behind you, over the ridge of Yar Tor, is Corndon Down. Drop down from your stance, go over the ridge and cross the dark, dry and shallow valley between the tor and the down. On your left are the attractive upland farmsteads of Sherwell and Babeny, embraced by their small, green and stone-walled fields, and ahead is the smooth curve of the top of the down, interrupted by two or three seeming granite tors. Head downhill, pass just to the right of the drystone walls, and then step up again towards the left-hand 'tor'. This is your last uphill tramp of the day! The seeming 'tor' is man-made and very old, a vast Bronze Age burial cairn. Follow the path south along the spine of the down to another cairn, at 434m. From this granite crown look back, at Sharp Tor and at Yar Tor. You are just above Corndon Tor, scattered across the contour lines 30m below. The walk has one more surprise. Descend south-west, back to your car. Close to the road is a memorial cross. Pause and decipher the words, and then look up to Sharp Tor. Reflect on the courage of a 19-year-old officer killed gallantly leading his men in Palestine in 1918: *"... pro patria mori"*. You have enjoyed another lovely Dartmoor day: would that Lieutenant Cave-Penney had lived to share such.

The memorial cross to Lieutenant Cave-Penney, with Sharp Tor visible directly behind it.

Author

Summer

5. Hound Tor & Greator Rocks

6. Pupers Hill, Snowdon & Ryder's Hill

7. Heckwood Tor, Vixen Tor, Feather Tor & Pew Tor

8. Bellever Tor, Laughter Tor & Riddon Ridge

9. Little Mis Tor & Great Mis Tor

10. Birch Tor, Hookney Tor & Hameldown Tor

11. Rippon Tor, Hay Tor & Saddle Tor

Vixen Tor

G.Thurlow

─── 5. Hound Tor & Greator Rocks ───

Start and finish: SX 740792
Distance: 2.5km (1½ miles)
Approximate time: 2 hours

Holidaymakers are wary of Devon's narrow lanes with their tall earth and granite hedges, and their laughably tight 'passing places' which seem to have been built in about 1958 with Austin 7s in mind. The local drivers, on the other hand, adopt a world-weary air as they weave their way between the visitors' stationary vehicles. Admittedly the visitors are freighted with their families, and their careful progress around blind bends and past concealed farm entrances, through inky shade and blinding sunlight, is sensible but slow. They are understandably nervous of the elderly and battered local cars.

All the more reason then at the height of the holiday season to make an early start, especially when the required car park is nearly 4 miles from the main road, down a narrow, winding and shadowy lane. You will quickly establish if you are early enough: on a Sunday morning you may meet the occasional communicant nipping off to church, but otherwise the road should be empty and enable you to admire the tangled shape of Hound Tor from Swine Down quite quickly. From there, it is then only a few minutes drive to the car park below the tor, but even at 8a.m. you are unlikely to have it to yourself. It is, nevertheless, a secure car park as Dartmoor goes and, from later in the morning, enjoys the benefit of a first class mobile cafe – 'The Hound of the Basket Meals'.

Walk straight up the gentle hill towards the right-hand side of the rocks standing dramatically on the skyline. Hound Tor is not this prominent from a distance. Viewed from somewhere like Haytor, which is 61m higher, these bold rocks appear dwarfed by the green Devon countryside, but do not be deceived, as they form one of the largest and most dramatic rock formations on the moor. The tor looks especially impressive in mist, when changes in the light and perspective magnify its size and further distort its already chaotic appearance. This is a good tor: it is high, wide and split into several distinctive blocks of massive granite, and access is easy with little of the clitter which threatens unprotected ankles around so many other Dartmoor peaks.

At the right-hand end of the rocks turn left and walk easily upward on the soft turf 'avenue' sliced through the centre of the tor. On either side the grey rock towers above you: on the left the 'Hound Face' is a broken wall of granite blocks, on your right is the 'Central Block', a tall pyramid of slabs and vast boulders. The top of each is accessible with a little effort, and the view will make it worthwhile, especially on a summer morning. Make your way

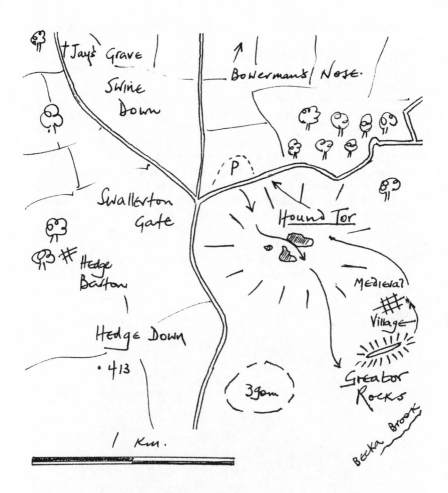

carefully up the warm dry rock and enjoy the sensation of firm rough granite under your finger tips as you use your hands to brace for balance as you progress. At the summit your first sensation should be one of light, then of a summer wind, but the last and strongest should be one of silence. It will be too cool still for insects to take to the wing, and animals and birds, awake since dawn, may already be resting until they are disturbed by men. Below you the trees are in full summer leaf, a sea of green treetops washing around cottage roofs and swirling up the narrow Dartmoor valleys. Higher still, the hilltops are burnt brown and yellow by the summer, and above them all lies this almost tangible silence, worn lightly under the empty blue sky.

The car park will now be filling up. Older families, or couples walking their dogs, will be picking their way slowly up the hill towards the tor.

Descend carefully from your airy position into the shade and then step up to the end of the 'avenue', from where the land drops away quite steeply to the Becka Brook, out of sight to the east. Between you and the brook lie your next two objectives: Greator Rocks and the medieval village. Greator Rocks will look black against the morning sun as you stroll down the hill and leave the remains of the village on your left for later. Follow the indistinct and uncertain path through pliant and green summer bracken towards the western edge of the little granite ridge, but head past the steep end of the rocks and walk on to a position from where you can see its sunlit southern flank. With luck, the sweeping wall will be painted with the purple of different heathers, as well as the white of granite and the green of whortleberry and heath. Behind you the first visitors will just be visible on Hound Tor, but here you will be alone.

This walk takes you along the crest of the ridge. The formation is unique on Dartmoor, a long, narrow and rocky ridge falling steeply away on either side to the moorland below, a miniature of Welsh mountain ridges which, like them, calls for delicate footwork and commands some lovely views. Step back towards the steep western edge of the ridge and choose your own way up on top: demanding or easy as inclination or skill allow. In all the years that I have

The long, narrow and rocky ridge of Greator Rocks.

Author

26

scrambled along this ridge I have never met another party, whether to give way or to overtake, and yet of all the special challenges and pleasures which the moor has to bestow this must be amongst the best.

Below, to your right, is the little valley of the Becka Brook. Sixty metres above is Haytor, dark and imposing on the southern skyline. In the sunlit air between, a buzzard turns and mews, and the strong hot breeze is heavy with the scent of heather and shrubs. On a warm summer morning this could be the Mediterranean.

Make sure that the waistbelt of your rucksack is tight and then choose your way carefully along the ridge, using your hands for balance. Step across from pinnacle to pinnacle, or weave your way between them, but take time to stop and admire the views to left and right and, close by, the rowan in berry and the dwarf oaks clinging to the gullies. Halfway along the ridge the path drops to a little col, and on the other side ascends to the left to rejoin the ridge top. Continue along to a large pyramid-shaped boulder: step past it and then stop for coffee.

When you can tear yourself away descend to the moor floor and walk down to the deserted 'village'. It is very small, more a farmstead or settlement, but what a delightful place to have lived. It is mentioned in Domesday as the Manor of Hundatora, and was occupied continuously until the 14th century, when either the Little Ice Age or the Black Death ended it all. What you see is the result of archaeological work in the 1960s, which laid bare the foundations of homes, byres and barns.

Then walk steadily uphill, past Hound Tor and the increasing trickle of visitors, to your car.

The northern part of the medieval village, with Hound Tor on the skyline.
Karen Lang

—— 6. Pupers Hill, Snowdon & Ryder's Hill ——
(A cautionary tale)

Start and finish: SX 694672
Distance: 8km (5 miles)
Approximate time: 2¹/₂ hours

The school atlas gives western Europe a maritime climate, without extremes, neither too hot nor too cold, washed by moist westerly airstreams and encompassed by swiftly-changing skies. Dartmoor's maritime aspect is created by the Atlantic, and the same grey-green weather, which draws curtains of mist and rain across the cold white-breaking seas of the Western Approaches, smothers the dark grey bulk of the Devon uplands and slicks the granite in quarry, tor and drystone wall. Then the North Hessary Tor mast vanishes, mist moves remorselessly down from the hilltops, only sometimes breaking to reveal a dark hillside before enveloping the closer slopes, and the occasional spatter of wind-driven rain is suddenly replaced by steady, penetrating drizzle.

Although you will occasionally be caught out, this is not walking weather by choice. It may, of necessity, be so if time is short and the empty moor beckons, and it is the reason why you will always carry your compass and map when walking in upland Britain. It is rarely life-threatening, as there are many roads around and through the moor to which to escape, but such weather can turn an evening stroll into something of an 'epic'. For those unfamiliar with the term, an 'epic' always involves unplanned risk-taking, some associated nervous excitement, and almost invariably wet feet, torn clothing and a long walk! Devonshire locals exercising their dogs on the edge of Dartmoor of an evening have been snared by mist close to home, and lost their way on familiar ground.

However, even in mist Dartmoor is an interesting place, and provided that you are competent, and have planned your escape routes, such weather is worth dressing up for. What follows is a cautionary tale on how not to do it ...

The south-east quadrant of the moor, between Venford Reservoir and Ugborough Beacon, is approached through the lovely valleys and small lanes of Holne, West Buckfastleigh and Dean Prior. The watercourses are small: the Holy Brook, the River Mardle, the Dean Burn and the Harbourne River drain the slopes between the Dart and the Avon. There is no easy parking around here, so choose your starting point with care and do not obstruct field gates or hamper access for the larger farm vehicles such as milk lorries and horse-boxes. But once your car is secure a spot such as Cross Furzes or in the lane leading to Lud Gate provides a quiet and elevated starting point for a good tramp into the heart of the southern moor.

Part of the lane leading to Lud Gate.

Author

Lud Gate is approached along a lovely stone-walled lane, typical of those which provide rough access between the public highway and the unfenced grazing around the moor. Beech trees provide shelter on either side, their leaves trembling in the strong south-westerly breeze, and late foxgloves bend under the weight of their tall slim stems and few remaining flowers on the moss-covered granite walls. The lane ascends gently, gaps between the trees providing clear views of the hills beyond with their crests already lost to view in low cloud. The world is composed of cool greys and greens: and even in midsummer there is no direct sunlight. The low cloud is a light grey, becoming almost white overhead, and the hills are a darker tone, their features merging so that navigation by eye is already growing uncertain. The trees are heavy with their summer foliage and the damp grass is verdant after a wet spell.

If you decide to proceed under these conditions there is a final check to be made before setting off from the car: have you got a compass, notebook and map? Without a compass this is what can happen ...

At Lud Gate pause and set the map, looking west to identify the closest features. Left to right are Hickaton Hill and Pupers Hill but, beyond them to

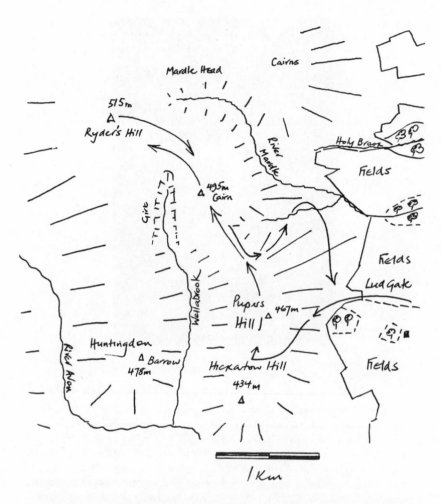

the north-west, the higher ground is shrouded in low cloud. There is a clear track ahead which leads to Huntingdon Warren, and by following this, even without a compass, the way back will, initially, be quite easy. Fold the map carefully because it is difficult to handle in the breeze: Hickaton Hill is already topped by a banner of mist spreading quickly downhill. The first ascent, to the left flank of Pupers Hill, is easy, picking a well-worn way past sheep, gorse with its occasional late blaze of yellow, and lonely little stunted trees. On higher ground, and looking back, any distant view is blurred by mist, and only the nearer moorland perimeter of enclosing field walls and woods stands out. Once on the ridge, there is a tantalising glimpse of Huntingdon Warren hill before it is curtained by mist, and then a distinct path turns right to ascend

Pupers Hill. There is still reason to be confident of the escape route, using the clear path and track and the slope of the land back down to the starting point. Mist has rolled down further, and continuous fine rain is borne in by the warm south-west wind. The top of Pupers Hill is just visible ahead and, behind, the path down to the Huntingdon Warren track is visible, but Hickaton Hill has disappeared along with the world of lanes and valleys around Holne and Combe. Pupers, incidentally, is said to mean 'Pipers', as in 'Pied Piper', and the rocks to be the stone remains of legendary delinquent musicians!

The view eastwards from the slopes of Pupers Hill – on a clear day!

Author

The cairn at the top of Pupers Hill may be the last fixed point in a world of shifting visibility, so close study of the well-folded map is essential. There is a path shown from here to Snowdon, a kilometre northwards, with level walking marked by cairns, and beyond is Ryder's Hill, at 515m the high point of this area. A deliberate pause may be rewarded with a brief parting of the curtain of mist so that the relationship of Ryder's Hill to Snowdon can be seen: at the same time sunlight breaks through over the summer countryside below, and a hazy landscape of golden and green patchwork swims into view, before the light is dramatically extinguished and the fields sink once more out of sight. Confident of the retreat, and having seen both Snowdon and Ryder's Hill ahead, it is possible to follow the indistinct track in the direction of the cairns, which are out of sight and a kilometre to the north. It is, in fact, 500 double paces across level moorland, with the land sloping away to the right to nearby fields and footpaths. Halfway there the mist lifts briefly and the low cairns come into sight: beyond them is nothing but a grey curtain drawn closely to the heath.

At the cairns, without a compass, the correct route is back and off the hill to find a cup of tea! The world is grey and wet. The cairns on Snowdon are aligned pointing back along the sheep track to Pupers Hill and the car. Ahead is silence. However, the alignment of the cairns provides a pointer forwards as well as back, and there are no dangers, cliffs or gorges between Snowdon's last cairn and Ryder's Hill, 500 double paces ahead. This is a cautionary tale ...

There is no path. 500 double paces lead apparently into emptiness, with visibility down to about 15 metres. On each side the green moss is brushed by ripening yellow grasses, bent by the steady wet wind, their seed-heads dipping and dripping with beads of mist. Occasional sheep tracks meander in and out of vision, and underfoot the ground changes slowly from heath to bog and back to heath. Aiming off slightly to the right to intersect with Mardle Head and to avoid Wellabrook Girt, at last, after 300 double paces, the ground steepens as it should. A path of sorts comes in from the left, heading up in the same direction, and then looming out of the mist is a group of figures. Sheep perhaps?

Gradually the group hardens into a trig point and a boundary stone. Our destination! After 500 double paces the stones must be approached carefully, so that the return route can be clearly fixed. Once at the trig point, a few turns by the incautious visitor and every downward slope or path will seem the same, with the directions indistinguishable. The difference between east and west at this point is critical. Eastwards there are fields and paths downhill within 2¹/₂km. But westwards it is 9km of barren moorland to Burrator Reservoir. Here, there are no views, only a circle of cloud with a 20-metre radius.

The retreat from Ryder's Hill (also known as Petre's Bound Stone as it marked the edge of Sir William Petre's 16th century estates in Brent) is straightforward, although a brief glimpse of Wellabrook Girt through the rain reveals more of a hazard under these conditions than the map indicates ... The girt and Gibby Beam (harsh-sounding names for hard work) are the remains of tin workings. With relief, the cairns on Snowdon reappear after just over 480 double paces, and the way home is clear. Or should be ... More problems are experienced on the way down from a hill than on the way up. Whether from delight at a successful piece of ascent, or from tiredness, now is the time for map-reading errors to occur, and a mistaken early descent from Snowdon plunges into a pathless stretch of bracken and streams which bears no relationship to the map. Casting around for features which fit the walker's perception of the land, leads the unwary to Buckfastleigh Moor and Scorriton Down, until half an hour later, hot, cross and with bootlaces plucked at by heather, the truth finally dawns ... a whole kilometre out! Fortunately, in this case, the mist has lifted and the route home is a short uphill plod.

There are three morals to this tale: firstly never go out without your map and compass; secondly beware of the descent; and, thirdly, Dartmoor, even in the mist, is worth your time.

7. Heckwood Tor, Vixen Tor, Feather Tor & Pew Tor

Start and finish: SX 535728
Distance: 5km (3 miles)
Approximate time: 1¹/₂ – 2 hours

Early morning, when the sun is still low above the haze, or when the land is hugged by a drifting blanket of mist, is the best time of day. A pale light slants across tor and combe, and the colours of grass and gorse are enhanced through refracted dew. Later in the day the high sun bleaches out all colour and washes away the shadows, but, in the morning light, gorse burns with a brilliant flame and every hollow and every crest is lit with careful precision; added to which you will have this lovely world to yourself because everyone else is still in bed! Of course, you needn't be too self-righteous; you could be positively penitential and rise early (very early) in midsummer, but you can be out on the hill at 9.30a.m. on an autumn Sunday and the effect will be roughly the same – an empty moor and traffic-free roads all suffused with the crystal light of a newly-made day. Once, above Widecombe, scrambling amongst the silent sunlit little ridges of Chinkwell Tor, we were stopped by the melody of church bells drifting gently up the valley of the East Webburn.

On such a morning you should visit Vixen Tor. This large sphinx-like rock is a unique place. Tors ought to be on a hillcrest, but most of the routes to Vixen Tor involve a degree of descent, and from the Tavistock to Princetown road it seems to lie in a valley bottom. This is because out of sight from the road and beyond the tor lies the wooded Walkham Valley. Vixen Tor has another secret: despite its seemingly low position, the west side of the main rock offers the highest continuous face on the moor towards an afternoon sun. It is a handsome sight in the morning and at sunset.

Don't start your visit from the Princetown road unless you like swamps and the season has been reasonably dry, and only begin from Merrivale if you are purely tor 'bagging', as the path is dull and has no intrinsic attraction. This walk starts at Sampford Spiney. Park your car off the road near the track heading towards Pewtor Cottage. If there is no space there, and it is a tiny area, then head back in the direction of Pew Tor, where there is invariably somewhere to leave a car off the road, and walk back past the hunt kennels to Sampford Spiney.

Sampford Spiney is a lovely hamlet and an old parish, consisting of a church, a sloping mossy green cut by a slender brook, a Victorian schoolhouse (cottage), a very old farmhouse (rendered genteel by yew hedges) and a few large villas, all hung around with tall trees which shelter the gathered dwellings from the encroaching moorland. In days of old this parish represented the limits of life-sustaining human endeavour clinging to the edge of upland Dartmoor barrenness.

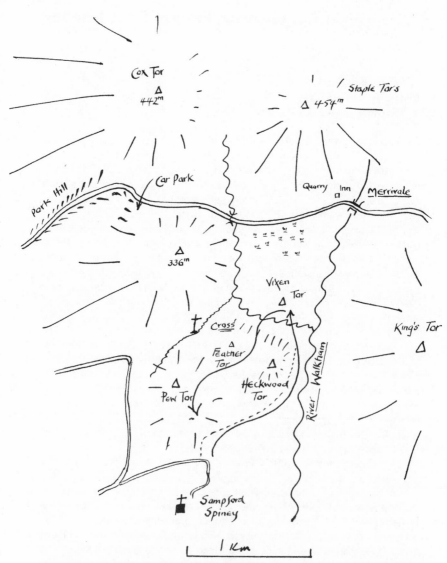

The track to Pewtor Cottage is surrounded by furze. Walk up it a little way and then look back, towards the pinnacles of Sampford Spiney's church tower, which are turreted amidst the dark green foliage of pine trees – a vivid contrast to the burning yellow patches of gorse close to hand. Step up on the sheep-nibbled turf to the right of the vehicle track and then head gently upwards on the narrow footpath towards Heckwood Tor. You join a small bridlepath and head eastwards beside the drystone wall, leaving behind Pewtor Cottage with its hedge of tall privet. Away to the right are the woods of the Walkham Valley, purple-brown with upheld empty branches in autumn, but heavy with their green harvest of leaves in summer and with the tumbling, fast-flowing salmon river silent and out of sight beneath the canopy. To your left skylarks rise from the heath: to your right buzzards patrol the treetops, and beyond and above them lie the rocks of King's Tor and the old Princetown railway track. Ahead of you is Heckwood Tor, a ridge of rocks cutting downhill from the left, and, as you step past them, there is a little quarry with abandoned dressed-granite blocks. The path slopes down and peters out on the edge of the wide and empty wetland bowl below Vixen Tor, cut by a stream which rises on the slopes of Cox Tor away to your left.

This is your first sight of the rock mass. The perspective across the vale provides one of the best internal views on Dartmoor. From the edge of Heckwood Tor you look squarely down at the high west face of the crag, at its three tightly-packed formations, and into the encircling drystone wall boundary which marks the perimeter of this small private estate. Out of sight, to the right, is the tiny Vixen Tor cottage, tucked close under the rocks, hidden by trees and marked only by a thin wisp of blue breakfast smoke. Nearer to hand, as you descend more steeply to cross the stream, is a scattering of rocks beyond the drystone wall, but your objective is the stile giving access to Vixen Tor, on the other side of the brook.

If you have left this walk until late in the day you may see small groups of walkers scattered across the moorland to your left, some on the move, others stationary: this is the heart of letterboxing country. If, however, you started out early enough you should be on your own: at most you will meet a young man running before breakfast.

Cross the chattering little stream as footwear and athleticism allow, and pick your way past puddles and pools of still water towards the gate and stile built into the wall; then enter the roughly circular enclosure. From here, where you are level with the base of the tor and looking at its summit rising above the trees and bushes beyond the low coping, you gain a truer sense of its height. It is possible to scramble to the top of each of the three blocks, but the easiest is the lowest, the one on the left. Walk through the bushes towards the crag and then head up its left flank, picking your way upwards through the boulders to the back, where the level ground is higher and the main rock, in consequence, appears less high. From here we want to get to the top. Vixen Tor's final secret is that it is one of the few moorland summits which cannot be reached without a technical climb! *But don't attempt it if a raven's nest is visible.*

You have a choice. The two higher rock groups are split by a narrow 'chimney': a dark and damp place. It is a wriggling, shoulder-jamming, heaving and pushing route to the top, with a final exhilarating jump from one granite block to the other and a marvellous view. There is no alternative easier

One of the two higher rock groups of Vixen Tor.

Author

route to the summit of Vixen Tor, but you do not need a rope. The alternative is the right-hand block (as viewed from the south) which is a simple scramble, made easier with a friend to extend, or be extended, the occasional hand. The views are delightful from all three of the tops. These are not big, breathtaking vistas: they are English, inner Dartmoor views, images best painted in amateur watercolours or by a skilled miniaturist, and that is why they are best enjoyed when the light is perfect. Morning is better than evening because the dawn's light usually inherits a clear night sky: by day, clouds build and sunset is more likely to be fragmented.

The rest of the morning need not be anti-climactic, especially if you have a brisk walk and a lunchtime glass in mind. Set aside the easy temptation of the Dartmoor Inn at Merrivale for another day and head west, back across the stile and stream towards a distinctive square block on the ridge of Heckwood Tor. If you are feeling energetic scramble up on top of the block and look north to the scattered rocks of Feather Tor: walk through them towards the stone cross beside the leat. Beyond are the small ledges on the edge of Barn Hill, worth a detour if you are letterboxing but otherwise only waymarks from the car park at the foot of Cox Tor.

Beckamoor Cross (The Windypost), near Feather Tor.

Karen Lang

Your route takes you back towards Pew Tor by following the leat but not giving up too much height before heading past a small quarry to the top of this wide-ranging rock formation. It is a popular destination for young families, dog owners and retired couples, walking and playing amidst the tumbled boulders and rearing crests. The wide view of the western skyscape and as far as Plymouth Sound brings lasting pleasure.

From here you can see your car and, depending on the time of day, you will anticipate either fresh coffee in Tavistock or a sparkling draught at the Whitchurch Inn. If you started really early the coffee will be great!

– 8. Bellever Tor, Laughter Tor & Riddon Ridge –

Start and finish: SX 656772
Distance: 6km (3³/4 miles)
Approximate time: 2 hours

The central moor is etched by pine forests – Fernworthy, Soussons, and Bellever – and each blankets the high ground of the moor with a clearly-defined perimeter. Some visitors find this regimented monoculture unsympathetic and unattractive, but undeniably such extensive stands of dark green timber, stretching across the sloping land, lend additional texture to the landscape. In much the same way artificial expanses of water in the moor's reservoirs bring a change of light to their surrounding hills.

The trees and the reservoirs are both marks of industry in this environment; both are a fair reflection of man's needs, and both are more benign than tin working and peat diggings. The forests stand in stark contrast with the deciduous woods, which cling haphazardly to steep-sided river valleys on the edge of the moor, but neither is intrinsically better or more attractive.

In combination with cascading water, sunlit rocks and warm and level grass such woodlands exert a strong influence on the human imagination, and where such a place is accessible to the public it is always popular. A site such as Bellever Bridge, with its well-hidden car parks, inevitably attracts visitors, and the starting point of this walk is always very busy on a sunny weekend or holiday. There is a youth hostel here, too.

This walk starts in the car park beside the River Dart at Bellever Bridge. Walk up the hill towards the forest, leaving the youth hostel on your right. You are walking on the Lich Way, an age-old footpath used for crossing these uplands and linking remote settlements, now waymarked by the Forestry Commission for visitors. It is steady uphill work on peaty ground, and once amongst the trees orientation can be surprisingly difficult: the map can be misleading, matching tracks through the forest with those shown on an older map can be very difficult, and felling can alter the shape of the forest dramatically. However, do stay on the tracks and do not be tempted to wander off into the shadows ... where it will be even easier to get totally confused!

On either hand tall firs march with the forest rides. From overhead, the narrow span of open sky lights the tree trunks alongside your path with their regular erect boles brushed by grey-green moss. Beyond them the columns of timber recede in shadowed ranks into the quiet dim half darkness. The tall trees absorb all sound. The silence is profound. Once you may hear the rasping alarm of a jay, cutting through the stillness without echo or reverberation.

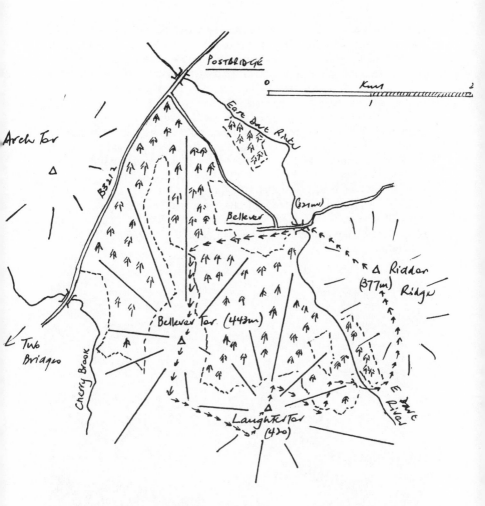

Underfoot, a dry branch of dead timber snaps, and where light penetrates through the dark green foliage above, the forest floor is a litter of tinder and branches. At an intersection, pick up the track for Dunnabridge.

The Forestry Commission has done much good work to preserve archaeological sites and one of the pleasures of Bellever (and other forests on the moor) is to come across a tiny glade, offset to one side of a ride, down an overgrown path. At the end, and lit from above through a gap in the encircling forest, is a tiny setting of granite stones, a kist or stone row closely guarded by a ring of dark trees. Very Tolkien.

The edge of the forest comes suddenly in a flood of light. The wind, outside the trees, sighs in their branches: light and noise in contrast with the dark and stillness within. Beyond the trees is a chaos of clear-felled land, of tree stumps surrounded by the debris of forestry – shattered grey branches, part trunks and a tangle of tinder. Further on again is the clear line of the next stand of trees, all of the same height, their tips a black perforation of the sky beyond. On a warm day, all around, is the scent of pines.

And ahead is the broad green path, steadily rising to the split granite summit of Bellever Tor, at 443m the summit of your walk and 140m above Bellever Bridge. The path is flanked at a distance by trees, and the horizon ahead is the tor itself, so the view from the top is as sudden as it is dramatic.

You are effectively in the middle of Dartmoor with a 360° panorama which sweeps from summit, to moorland, to forest, and back to moorland again. Climb up to the trig point and orientate your map with the features. It is obvious why this tor was, until the beginning of the 20th century, the meeting place for a May festival. On your left, and the next objective, is the delightfully-named Laughter Tor.

Laughter Tor.
Karen Lang

Descend south from the tor following the track for Dunnabridge. Below you, amongst the trees, is a white forestry track slashing the woods, while above, and to the right, on the hillside opposite, is your track faintly wandering through the heather and whortleberry. Continue downhill to the junction of walls, where there is a five-bar gate to your left and a stile to the right. Go through the gate and then follow the faint track, gradually rising to the right of Laughter Tor. On your right-hand side the southern moor's low flat curves swell gently upwards, purple and blue in the distance.

At the skyline, cut left to the top of the tor, which is low and flat, and a place where clitter and rocks are parted by a drystone wall and a wooden gate. Behind you Bellever Tor now looks striking, as does Yar Tor directly in front of you on the far side of the East Dart River, which itself is close by but out of sight. Elsewhere, being early summer, the landscape is painted in green contrasts – the forest in sombre dark tones – the fields in fresh brilliant hue – and the heath in worn and faded shades.

From Laughter Tor descend eastwards, keeping the wall close by on your left. Step through the gap in a drystone wall crossing your route (never climb over such walls) and then swing right, still dropping, until you join another track. Head left along this track, go through another gate and then into the scrub on the edge of the forest. From there, the Babeny path will lead you to the edge of the East Dart River below Laughter Hole House. (If you feel a twinge of envy when passing Laughter Hole Farm and House, do not feel alone!) Cross the river using the stepping stones. (This may be a torrent, but the stepping stones are substantial: if it has been raining heavily and the crossing is impassable, follow the path along the west bank of the river in order to return to Bellever Bridge.)

On the other side of the river it is time for a little exercise. Keeping the enclosure wall on your left, climb steeply up 100m to the top of Riddon Ridge, an area without the grandeur of a tor but the centre of a distant amphitheatre of hills. It is well worth the effort. From the 380m crest, walk easily north-west, heading gently back downhill towards Bellever Bridge. Eventually the river will come back into sight below, and you will almost certainly see children playing and parents enjoying the sunshine. Ahead is water, gorse in flower and the Forestry Commission's smart white-painted cottages. A very Dartmoor scene.

Bellever Bridge.
Author

——— 9. Little Mis Tor & Great Mis Tor ———

Start and finish: SX 553750
Distance: 5km (3 miles)
Approximate time: 2 hours

The best light falls across the moor in early morning and early evening. Then the combination of shadow and colour lends emphasis to the landscape and drama to the unfolding sky above. From high up on the western side of the moor the sunset seems especially vivid: an imperial canopy of purple and gold spread over an earthly vista of crimson, blue and grey. Such stirring horizons can be yours when the weather grants a clear western sky and if you have the courage to set out for the hilltops after supper in the middle months of the year. The mid-months are best, for if you linger on the hill there may be enough light to see you safe to the car park or the pub, as the stars come out behind you one by one.

This walk takes you up to the battlements of Great Mis Tor, which stands back from the Tavistock to Princetown road at a height of 538m, and dominates the moor to the north of Merrivale. The area is wealthy with archaeological sites: standing stones, stone rows, hut circles and kistvaens, to which the lengthening shadows of twilight lend both definition and romance.

Merrivale is on the southern edge of the Dartmoor military ranges. Do check beforehand that your visit will not be thwarted by large red army banners on every peak. This is a busy training area and the army publicises its use.

The walk starts in a little car park on the south side of the road just east of the bridge over the River Walkham. You are at an altitude of 320m, with about 200m of ascent ahead of you to the summit of Great Mis Tor, which is on the horizon directly in front of you. A little lower than the car park, and at the bottom of the valley, just below the quarry, the Dartmoor Inn has a good selection of refreshments for later in the evening.

Cross the road and follow the wall running uphill alongside the big enclosure beyond. This enclosure lies on the shallow eastern slope of the Walkham Valley and forms a private expanse of pasture, rocks and clitter. The hard, black granite drystone wall, on the other hand, stretches in a vast arc soaring across the slopes under Little Mis Tor, and is cut on its far side by a stream which runs across the enclosure from east to west. Make for this point and you will see that the stream cuts back into the slope on your right, its little natural valley deepened and widened by rudimentary tin-mining. When the alluvial tin deposits in the river below had been exhausted, the miners would have moved up the hillside to work the original metal lodes by using simple open-cast methods, and on Dartmoor the resultant gullies usually align east-west.

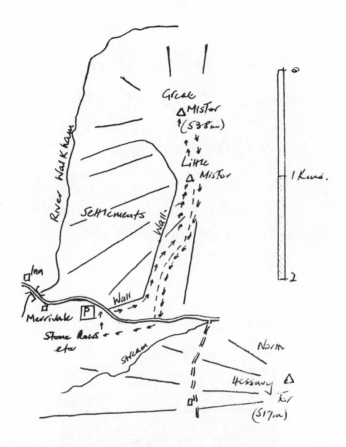

Lower down, within the enclosure, there are three blowing houses, a type of mill used extensively for smelting tin ore on Dartmoor until about 1750. Surrounding you are hut circles and enclosures dating from about 1750 BC, below you in the valley is Hillside Farm, and opposite is the big granite quarry. It really is a remarkable site. Here is a valley which has been in continuous productive agricultural use for over 3,500 years, and in continuous industrial use for probably the same length of time. The evidence is laid out on the ground before you. It is a humbling experience.

Look ahead now for Little Mis Tor, a four-square blockhouse of rock on the immediate horizon. It looks from this distance like an artificial construction. Cross the stream and, keeping the wall to your left, tramp up through the grass and heather with your lengthening evening shadow lying on the ground in front of you. Away behind, and to your left, the sun is growing a deep and ancient red.

The tor itself offers a pleasant scramble up the right-hand side for you to

Little Mis Tor.
Karen Lang

Great Mis Tor, viewed from the west.
Author

get to the top, and enjoy the views. You will notice a good-quality vehicle track behind the tor, which drops back down to the main road. Experience a glow of self-satisfaction! The hardest bit of the walk is over and it is only an easy stroll of under a kilometre, and 50m higher, to Great Mis Tor.

Great Mis Tor is an extensive formation with substantial outcrops to the west of the main summit. You can, if you wish, enjoy a number of scrambles of varying degrees of difficulty in and around the tor, with perhaps the easiest being immediately under the flag staff itself. Time, however, will be measured by the sun and you will end sitting quietly on the high western outcrop waiting for the day to die in western Cornwall, where waves of shadow, mist and purple break over successive hills and vales.

Take your time on the descent: rocks, heather and haste can quickly lead to twisted ankles. With daylight fading fast you can do without injuries! If you have time to spare then hurry down the military track, cross the main road and look at the double stone rows just above your parked car. In the low evening light their mystery is palpable.

Whether you have time for the stone rows or not, return to your car and head for the pub, as the last of the swallows call it a day, and as the stars commence their nightly round.

The double stone rows at Merrivale.

Karen Lang

−10. Birch Tor, Hookney Tor & Hameldown Tor−

Start: SX 675811
Finish: SX 721802 (or SX 675811)
Distance: 8 – 9km (5 – 5^1/2 miles)
Approximate time: 2 hours

The north-eastern moor is a contrast to the west. Less rugged, more rolling; less gorse, more heather; less gold, more purple. The hills billow smoothly upwards, their flanks curving steeply from the narrow valleys which lie on either side of the road west to Postbridge. This is a softer and more tranquil face of Dartmoor, where human settlement seems to have penetrated deeper and higher in valley and combe. The continuity of life is measured by sites at prehistoric Grimspound, the deserted medieval village at Hound Tor, the longhouses at Lettaford and West Coombe, the castle at Gidleigh, and the wealthy houses of Edwardian England. It was also marked by industrial activity. The Vitifer and Birch Tor tin mines opposite the Warren House Inn were the largest on the moor, and the inn, with its legendary hearth, would have made good profits. This high land around the inn is also a watershed. To the north rise the Teign and the Bovey: to the south run the West and East Webburns. Neither have the cachet of major rivers but, together, give the walker an entrancing cross-section of upland England, their waters separated by the north-south ridges of Birch Tor and Hamel Down.

There is a small car park 100m north-east of the inn, but this route could be a one-way walk and you may need to make arrangements to be met on the other side of Hamel Down.

From the road a stony track descends to the valley below. Away to the right is the regimented forestry plantation of Soussons Down, an extensive stand of resin-scented pines, and on the closer open hillsides are a number of large enclosures. As you drop to the stream, through the tailings from the two tin mines, stop and listen. Listen to the wind and the skylarks: wait. In this profound silence you may hear deeper noises: water and rock underground.

Cross the stream, follow the watercourse a little way, and turn left immediately beyond the foundations of a derelict mine building to pick your way up 110m of ascent to the summit of Birch Tor. The effort will warm you up in preparation for the rest of the walk and stretch your calf muscles. At the top the tor is an undistinguished assembly of massive broken granite, with pleasant views south into small green valleys, east to Hookney Tor on the far side of the intervening stream, and back to the Warren House Inn. Just below the hill is a shallow col which divides it from the 460m hill of Challacombe Down – a kilometre to the south and having another small enclosure on its

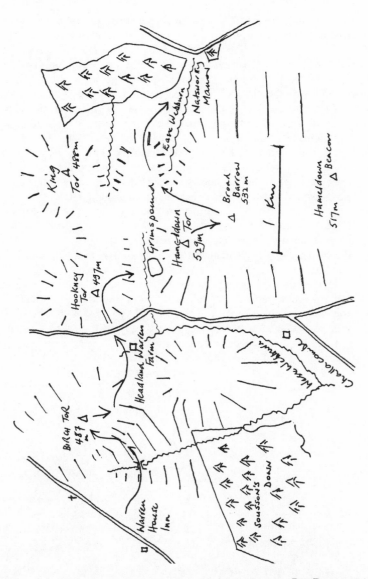

lowest slope as well as a much-restored stone row close by. But Dartmoor is a landscape of contrast and during the walk you may be reminded that, in addition to archaeologists, the area is regularly used by low-flying military aircraft. You are not so high that they can suddenly appear below you, as in Snowdonia or Scotland, but you are high enough to watch them through a wide arc of skyscape, sun glinting on cockpits and thunder trailed over the land.

Drop down into the little col and rejoin the broad path for a short descent to Headland Warren Farm, and a new valley. The warren surrounds you, a disused breeding area for farmed rabbits: it is one of many on Dartmoor, some of which date back to medieval times. The farm looks south down a lovely valley, which is sheltered from the north by the ridge of East Bovey Head at 451m, and from the east by Hamel Down. In the north of England such a gentle fold of land would be distinguished by the title 'dale' but here, remote from Scandinavian influences, it is nameless on the map. Downstream, a little over a kilometre further south, is the hamlet of Challacombe, reduced to a single farm, and above it the slopes of Challacombe Down. The 'lynchets' on the slopes of the valley are medieval terraces of plough land and provide more evidence of the slow, but continuous, flow of human activity in this remote little community. In May you will hear a cuckoo and at all times you will be welcomed by the farm dog, its bark the only other sound as you pass to the left of Headland Warren Farm, cross over the brook, and take a path towards the road. Cross, trending to the left of Hookney Tor.

On the other side of the road find a path through the heather and follow it, gaining 80m up the north-west flank of the tor to its summit. Suddenly, at the peak, the view opens to include the col which connects Challacombe with the next north-south valley, and in the col lies the four-and-a-half acre Grimspound, one of the largest of the Bronze Age sites. With a massively-constructed wall and entrance, the impressive pound shelters a group of Bronze Age hut circles. Step down the broad granite-stepped path to the site, walk through to the far side and then ascend Hameldown Tor (529m) to the

Grimspound and Hameldown Tor, from Birch Tor.

Karen Lang

trig point and the summit cairn. *Do not be tempted to add a stone.* You are now on a broad ridge which runs from King Tor, to the north-east, seven kilometres southwards to Wind Tor and Widecombe, its spine traced by a level path of black peat which runs due south along Hamel Down, connecting successive barrows and culminating at Hameldown Beacon. In between the large barrows are cairns and lesser barrows, one of which yielded a richly-decorated amber dagger pommel studded with gold pins, which lasted thousands of years only to be destroyed in the bombing of Plymouth.

Underfoot the peat is scored by boot marks, while around you the wind sighs and plucks at your clothing. To the west is a vast panorama of receding moorland hillcrests, interleaved with a hundred shades of grey and blue. Seemingly close by on your left are Hound Tor and Hay Tor, but that view is, in part, obscured by the near horizon of the ridge on which you are walking. Walk to Broad Barrow and arrive on the summit at 532m, after an hour and half of steady tramping from the Warren House Inn. You are standing on part of the Two Moors Way, a north-south footpath along the eastern side of the moor which you could, if you wished, follow to Hameldown Beacon before dropping down to Challacombe and then heading back to the Warren House Inn through the forest on Soussons Down.

But this walk is in the opposite direction and heads just east of north. Pick a route through the level heath, following a succession of narrow sheep trails where the heather tugs at your bootlaces, and steadily diverge from the peat footpath on your left. Avoid the steep valley at the head of the East Webburn River, on your right, and head in the direction of King Tor, which you can use as a leading mark ahead when it comes into sight. After about a kilometre you will intersect a bridlepath; turn right and head downhill.

This path takes you into another aspect of Dartmoor. As you descend you could be anywhere: Snowdon, Scotland or the Lakes. On your right the steeper ground of the East Webburn Valley cuts back into the ridge. Around you the ground slopes down to a peaceful pine-forested valley which runs north-south across your front. And beyond is a landscape of contorted ridges, rows of breaking waves, their frozen crests dark blue in the haze and marked by the rocks of Bonehill, Chinkwell Tor, Honeybag Tor, Hay Tor, Rippon Tor and Hound Tor.

But this is Dartmoor, not Scotland, and these are not mountain vistas, nor are they mountain distances! Very quickly the path brings you down to the woods at Natsworthy Manor, where the trees are mixed fir and beech, grey drystone walls line the narrow road, and the shallow stream chuckles between low green banks. Overhead the buzzards maintain their eternal vigilance. I have counted seven in the sky hereabouts.

It is a pastoral spot in which to stop for a cup of tea beside silent stone walls, murmuring pine trees and trickling water, and with luck you have arranged for a car to meet you. If not, then you could retrace your steps back to the Warren House Inn, where you could plan to meet the Transmoor Link bus, a service which operates during the summer.

—— 11. Rippon Tor, Hay Tor & Saddle Tor ——

Start and finish: SX 742760
Distance: 4km (2^1/2 miles)
Approximate time: 1^1/2 hours

There are some places on Dartmoor which are instantly recognisable and which have been an essential part of the visitor's itinerary since Victorian times. They always feature in colour calendars of West Country scenes and were once the repeated subject of poster artists' brushes for tourist board advertisements. Hay Tor, with its commanding position on the south-east moor, is such a place. It is a natural attraction; the rock is massive, the views are lovely and it is close to the picture-postcard village of Widecombe. The high rocks bear the remnants of an iron ladder which presumably once enabled ladies in long skirts and bustling petticoats to reach the top, and the nearby road is now scarred by car parks which are always popular. So it is inevitable that on a Sunday afternoon the grassy slopes are busy with families, young people in trainers and the elderly taking the air, and that the rock faces are cobwebbed with the blue and red ropes of the modern climber. It is a gentle scene which has probably been repeated decade after decade ever since the railway first brought visitors to Devon, with only the changes in dress reflecting the changes in fashions and the passage of time. It is the ideal place for a stroll, either after lunch or before supper, and this route takes only an hour and a half or so, unless you are distracted by the views or pause to watch the climbers.

The walk takes in Rippon Tor, Hay Tor and Saddle Tor, three different and attractive rock formations in close proximity just east of Widecombe. The appearance of this area of the moor has more in common with the peaks and steep slopes of the northern moor than with the smooth and featureless expanses of the south. The hills and valleys encircling these three tops also embrace Hound Tor, Greator Rocks, Honeybag Tor, Chinkwell Tor and Bonehill Rocks, each one attractive and, together, forming a landscape of contrast with the sharp individuality of the granite rocks and the gentle beauty of the surrounding valleys.

The walk to the top of Rippon Tor does not really prepare you for this. It is a steady, even dull, ascent up an easy slope and following a little-used path through the expanse of brown heather, the air still and warm on a calm summer afternoon and with a grey haze settled on the near horizon. From the trig point at the top, and from nearby cairns, the view to the south-east looks out over the Teign Estuary and to the iron of the distant Channel. Close by, the countryside of the South Hams is vividly lit by a sunburst through the haze, gold-white light gleaming over distant field and hedgerow before fading back

into the summer haze. Inland, Hay Tor dominates the foreground with, in the middle distance, the dragon-back scarp of Greator Rocks to its left and then Hound Tor, misleadingly unimpressive. The cairns are Bronze Age burial barrows, and the slopes to the south-east are marked by ancient settlements. Of more modern date, and just below the summit rocks on the north-west slopes of the tor, is an interesting recumbent slab of granite with a cross cut in relief, while nearby are what would appear to be unfinished millstones.

Drop steeply down to the drystone wall which runs across the lower slopes of Rippon Tor and cross the wall by one of the few obvious gaps, readily identified by the footpaths on each side. Don't cross anywhere else: a drystone wall is easily damaged and they are an essential part of the English upland landscape. Beyond the wall the path quickly peters out in the heather, so pick your own way down towards the road before crossing over directly beneath the southern slopes of Saddle Tor. Leave that tor until later and, instead, head towards Hay Tor, keeping the road on your right and following the obvious path over the shoulder of Saddle Tor until the bulk of Hay Tor is visible. As you swing across the intervening sward Hay Tor grows steadily in size. Although only 457m above sea level and, therefore, a relatively low tor, it rises a sheer 30m from its base and stands as one of the largest and most

The north-western slopes of Rippon Tor, showing, in the foreground, the recumbent slab of granite with a cross cut in relief.

Karen Lang

impressive rock masses on the moor. A short steep rise brings you to the base of the first peak, Lowman, with Highman in front of you. Make your way to the top of Highman, giving space to the belayed leaders bringing up their seconds on the routes up the western face, and take in the steep drop on this side of the tor and the wide view into this lovely area of the moor. Immediately in front is a level stretch of heath running to the abandoned quarries, but just beyond is the Becka Valley: rising further west are the gently rising crests of successive hills breaking like waves into the heart of Dartmoor.

Drop down from Hay Tor away from the road and pass under the steep high face of Lowman into the wash of bracken. Away to your right are the spoils from quarries which were worked for the granite in the first half of the 19th century. London streets were paved with granite, not gold! Stroll comfortably towards Saddle Tor, increasingly aptly-named as you get closer, and walk up into the seat. From the outcrops on your right look out once more over the little Becka Valley and across its encircling Dartmoor country swathe of small fields and little woods.

That is the best of the walk. From here it's down to the metalled road and the traffic, and back to your waiting car to join the other families making their way off the moor and home.

Autumn

12. **Longstone Hill, Yes Tor & High Willhays**

13. **Fur Tor**

14. **Bell Tor, Chinkwell Tor & Honeybag Tor**

15. **Crow Tor & the Beardown Tors**

Crow Tor

G Thurlow

— 12. Longstone Hill, Yes Tor & High Willhays —

Start and finish: SX 562917
Distance: 8km (5 miles)
Approximate time: 2^1/$_2$ hours

Yes Tor and High Willhays comprise the highest point of Dartmoor, and various claims are made for their altitude (620m) when compared to other upland areas in the country. Such claims are boastful: reference to, for example, Ingleborough as the next highest peak (about 100m higher) rather overlooks the eminence of Snowdonia, but they do remind us that Dartmoor is the largest wild area in the otherwise overpopulated south of England, and that it is, therefore, worthy of our especial care and protection. The ground surrounding High Willhays and Yes Tor is well inside the army's exercise areas, and the easiest route to the top starts from the road close to their camp at Okehampton. Check that it is not a firing day!

It is arguable that the best environmental agency for the moor is the army, and that the worst damage is done here, as in the Pennines and elsewhere, not by Government or by predatory landowners, but by the unwitting general public who, one-at-a-time and in our thousands, vibram sole by vibram sole, widen the pathways and erode the peat. It is still a shock, however, to discover that the northern moor contains a military ring road, penetrating deep into the bowl formed by Hangingstone Hill, Cosdon Beacon and High Willhays, and on which you will occasionally spot a saloon car, complete with family picnic, tea cosies and nodding dog.

For all these reasons this route starts from the west, from the reservoir at Meldon and the car park there near the dam. A stretch of water lends enchantment to the landscape, especially on sunlit days when the gleaming fragment of fallen 'glass' seems cupped in the hands of the surrounding hills. Meldon Reservoir is no exception, and there are pleasant walks along the western side of the lake, heading towards the Sourton Tors and Sourton, which take you past mature trees and along almost level footpaths. The A30 is out of earshot to the north and the skylarks sing.

This walk, however, heads along the eastern side of the lake, where the prospect is altogether bleaker and where, on the land higher up, there are few obvious points of reference in mist. Like all decent mountain walks your objective on this route is generally concealed by the lower slopes, so a compass and map are useful.

Turn left out of the car park and head down to the reservoir, crossing the dam top to the far side. With each step you should shed another family, or a couple in trainers or welly boots, and on the far side of the dam you will almost

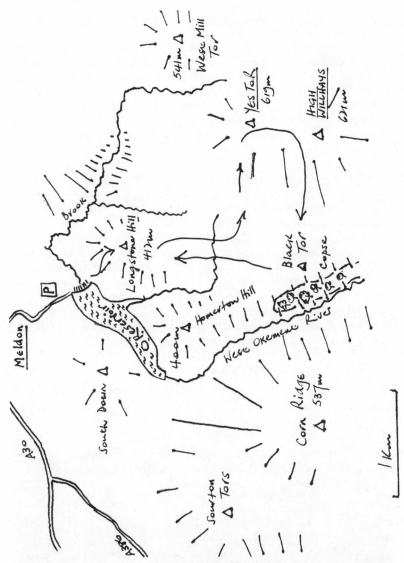

certainly be on your own. The metalled path runs out almost immediately. There is a way around the lake which follows the steep ground edging the shoreline, tracing a route around the single narrow inlet and then on to the footbridge at Vellake Corner, but it is frankly tedious! Instead, pick up the track which bends back towards the north-east and head steadily up towards the crest of Longstone Hill, overlooking the Red-a-ven Brook. From there the path swings to the right (south) and reaches a height of 400m – still 200m lower than your destination which is just over a kilometre away to the south-east.

In mist or poor visibility hold to the track until you can pick up a clear cross fix, either on one of the minor watercourses coming off Yes Tor, or until the track starts descending towards Black Tor. At either of these points pick a good compass bearing of 090 or higher, and cut loose across the heather for the top. It is a rough, steep and pretty featureless ascent towards Yes Tor, not the higher, but surely more of a peak and certainly providing better views over the lowlands to the north and west than High Willhays to your right and to the south. From the top, where you are at 2,000 feet (in old money!), the land drops away sharply below to the Red-a-ven Brook and the West Okement River, with the sunlit green quilt of north Devon stretching away to the misty blue northern horizon. Deep into the county to the west, and beyond the invisible Tamar, lie Bodmin Moor and Cornwall. Close by, however, are signs of military occupation – small sheds and wheeled-vehicle tracks: they are the reasons why you should ascend from the west ...

Staying on the narrow plateau, head south to the slightly higher High Willhays, a somewhat less distinguished peak, but giving views out into the heart of the moor and its slowly shifting panorama of light, shade and shadow. From here drop down south-west to Fordsland Ledge, overlooking Black-a-tor Copse and the narrow valley of the West Okement River running down to Meldon. Admire the view. This is Dartmoor at its best – secret valleys and tumbling water; dwarf trees embraced by lichen and by moss. It is time to go home: stay high and head north to pick up the track on Longstone Hill heading back to the dam.

A view looking across the valley of the West Okement River towards Yes Tor and West Mill Tor (left).

Karen Lang

——————— 13. Fur Tor ———————

Start and finish: SX 537823
Distance: 12km (7^1/$_2$ miles)
Approximate time: 4^1/$_2$ hours

Fur Tor, in the heart of the north moor, is just about as remote as you can get on Dartmoor, in Devon, and in England! It is said that there is nowhere as far from a road anywhere else in the country. It is a good, big tor; a handsome mass of rock. And, at 572m, it is the ninth highest peak on the moor. It is, therefore, a worthy objective and, happily, it is a peak which rejoices in a suitably inspirational approach – through Tavy Cleave. Cleave is a Devon word which describes the dramatic passage of a river from the highlands to the lowlands, a deep slash through the granite edge of Dartmoor, steeply-scarped and noisy with the torrent writhing in its narrow bed. Tavy Cleave is probably the most striking.

After first checking that live firing will not be in progress on the Willsworthy and Okehampton military ranges on the day of your planned walk, you need to find your way through the hamlets of Horndon and Willsworthy in order to park on the edge of the moor. In autumn the hedges alongside the narrow lanes between the Tavistock to Okehampton road and the moor are full of sloes and blackberries, and the final roads rise up towards the blue and quiet sky as if you are approaching the sea, invisible and just ahead.

———————————————————————

Leave your car beyond the gate. Out of sight to your right, and beyond Nattor Farm, is the River Tavy. Ahead rise Ger Tor and Hare Tor, with a stretch of rough pasture lying directly in front of you with a swift-flowing leat to mark the upland boundary. Make your way up to the leat and follow it inland, passing under the slopes of Nat Tor and into sight of the river. As you walk into the moor the land draws in around you; the river valley narrows and the land rears up on either hand above the path, the leat and the ever-closer river below. On a sunny day it is a cheerful place, full of the noise of water and warm with light. On an autumn day it can be a dark place ...

Ger Tor towers on your left-hand side as you patiently follow the curves of the leat, with its crystal clear water running over the golden brown gravel bed. The top of the tor is 130m above the river, nearly 500 feet of steeply-rising ground. On this day it is a dark and gloomy crag, standing above a junction where the leat meets the river in a complex piece of hydro-engineering. This is the last trace of modern man as the path, such as it is, peters out. Beyond, the track picks its way uncomfortably up and down beside the water, over roots and rocks; steeply into tumbling rocky stream beds and out again into muddy little scarps. This is Tavy Cleave. It is a Wuthering

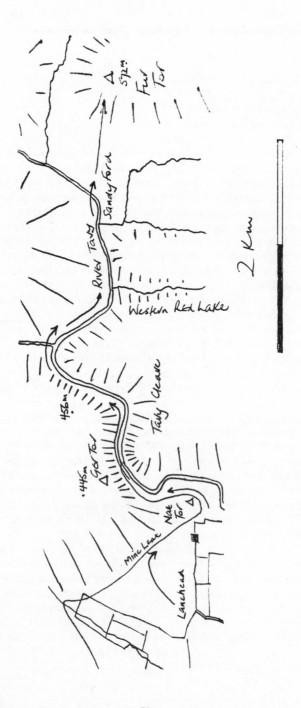

The approach to Tavy Cleave below Nat Tor.

Karen Lang

Heights sort of place which, we are told, has, in desolate winter blizzards, been choked with snow ... If you have the boots, the time and the strength it is well worth pushing steeply up to the top of the precipice (hands needed to ensure balance) so as to look down into the depths of this chasm.

As you step on, the river bed is rising; from 300m at the bottom entrance to the cleave to 390m where the main tributaries meet near the top. So, too, the slopes on either side are diminished as the river itself narrows and reduces in volume, tumbling over boulders, plunging into dark pools and careering past rocky islets. It is an exhilarating sight, and an ear-filling sound, second to none other on the moor. Finally, you emerge into the more open greener land where the Rattlebrook runs down from the north to join the Tavy. Cross it with care and stay on the north side of the river, heading south-east past the Bronze Age settlement of Watern Oke, one of the largest on the moor with nearly 100 huts. Across the river is the valley of the Western Red Lake, streaming from the heights opposite. Ahead, to the east, is Fur Tor: around you is the noise of the river and, above, the grey and cloud-tattered Dartmoor sky. This is the best place on earth!

Keep on until reaching Sandy Ford and then cross the Amicombe Brook to the southern bank, lying under Fur Tor. If needful then head higher up the brook to make the crossing dry-shod, but do not cross lower down. And then push on the next 1,500 steep and clitter-ridden metres to the top of Fur Tor and your objective for the day.

As William Crossing states in his *Guide to Dartmoor:*–

"Fur Tor is perhaps the grandest of the Dartmoor tors, for while there are some that rise much higher above the ground than the loftiest of the piles here, and also exhibit finer rock masses, there is none that covers so large an area, or whose surroundings are of the desolate character as those upon which this lonely tor looks down."

He adds that: "The larger masses of this tor form two distinct groups, one overlooking the great Amicombe Hill that extends away to the N., the other being E. of this, and nearer Cut Combe. We shall find the first on the brow of the hill, and shall notice that it consists of six piles of fairly large size and several smaller ones. From this we make our way across the level piece of ground, where rocks give place to grass and rushes, to the eastern group, which is the more important of the two. Here are four piles, the chief of which has a very striking appearance. On the highest part of it are three rock basins, one being so near the edge of the granite mass as to render the result of the action of the water in the wearing away of the stone visible from the ground. On the western side of this tor an immense block of granite will be observed overhanging, as it were, midway between the summit and the turf, and another similar block lies on the ground near by. The time must surely come when this immense stone will topple over; the tor is slowly going to ruin."

From this remote, high and wild position, with its wide and spacious views into the empty heart of the northern moor – extending to High Willhays and Yes Tor – it is tempting to press on inland. On this occasion, however, Fur Tor is the furthest point of the walk and it is now necessary to retrace your steps.

A distant view of Fur Tor from the north-west, which clearly indicates its remoteness in the heart of the northern moor.

Karen Lang

— 14. Bell Tor, Chinkwell Tor & Honeybag Tor —

Start and finish: SX 731775
Distance: 4km (2½ miles)
Approximate time: 1½ hours

When autumn comes the late season lays a cloak of russet across the gentle slopes of Dartmoor's uplands. The summer bracken dies and its new expanses of deep, almost glowing, brown illuminate the vivid green sward beneath. In the valleys 'gold dust' lies on the trees; here gilt, there ruddy; and the hedgerow blaze of colours is biased by the gothic green of the occasional holly, each shot through with a harvest of blood-crimson berries. Dartmoor is so far away from England's centres of population in London, the Midlands and even Bristol, that this warm out-of-season autumn face of the hills is one with which visitors are unfamiliar. Unlike the Peaks and Snowdon, which are quickly accessible from Liverpool and Manchester at any time of the year, Dartmoor is a long way down the M5. The Fall is, anyway, a chancy season: a visitor taking a weekend break to visit the moor is likely to find the hilltops swallowed by low cloud, the valleys full of water and the country lanes banked with sodden masses of dead leaves. An October storm puts the rivers in spate: fords become impassable and town bridges, once high above the pebbles, squat low above the deep, brown and roaring torrent. But on a blue autumn morning when there may have been a touch of frost, and a ridge of high pressure flows up the South West Approaches, then the fortunate visitor should head for Widecombe and leave that village by the narrowest and steepest of lanes to find Bonehill Rocks, Honeybag Tor and Chinkwell Tor: sonorous titles which describe a lovely ridge, seemingly high above the famous Dartmoor village and looking across the valley to the broad back of Hamel Down.

There is ample parking below Bonehill Rocks, from where you should cross the road and follow the path up towards Bell Tor, the first rocks on the ridge. You can walk easily up on the grass to the right of the rocks, but it is more fun to scramble up the right-hand side of the broad 'chimney' which splits the tor, ducking under the huge chockstone which forms an archway at the top, and then nimbly pick your way to the summit.

The view across the rooftops of Widecombe and its embracing patchwork of fields, woodland and moorland fulfils the spirit of autumn in all its misty glory, and will be the more so for having been found through a challenging route! When you can tear yourself away rejoin the easy path and walk north in the direction of Chinkwell Tor. After a little way, and before reaching its two cairns, head off to your left (there is no obvious path), giving up height

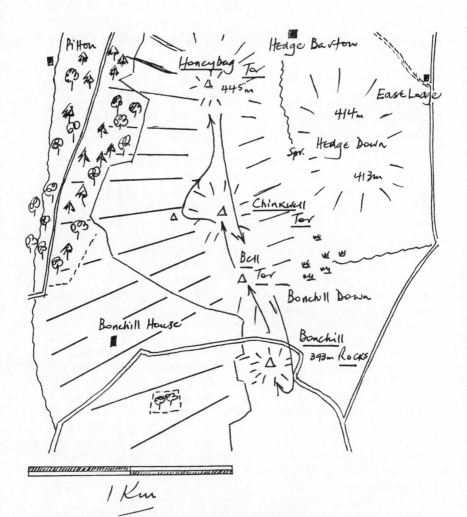

and dropping down a little way to the west. Keep your eyes open, and do not descend too far: you are looking for a large rock tower; a square bastion called *Widecombe Wall* which was very obvious looking upwards from within the village but not so up here approaching it from above.

I hope that you finally approach *Widecombe Wall* from above, and do not overshoot it on your descent. From behind, scramble up onto the top, over the two steps on the right, and then feel your way carefully to the front of the high and narrow scarp. The wall is a huge granite prow which cleaves the still air overlooking the East Webburn Valley, and there is a dizzy drop beneath you to the smooth turf immediately at its foot. If your walk is on a Sunday morning, and if you have timed it well, then the soft sound of ringing church bells will

Widecombe Wall, on the south-western slopes of
Chinkwell Tor.   *Author*

reach you from St Pancras's tower lower down and far away to your left. Step
down again with care – the two rock steps are quite exposed – and then walk
back up to visit the two cairns. From there look away to the east, towards
Hound Tor and Hay Tor. In contrast with the steep slopes behind you, the
world lies level and with a low autumn sun glinting on the wet land, a snail's
silver tracery of gleaming roads and glittering pools.

Immediately north, over a small saddle, lies Honeybag Tor, the limit of this
short stroll. Drop briefly down into the col and ascend the south side of the tor,
scrambling to the top at 445m. It is a tremendous, airy, place, commanding the
steep and narrow valley of the East Webburn where it rushes past the high dark
slopes of Hamel Down. Further north the valley becomes a more gentle
patchwork of autumnal woodland colours, worked through the bland swathes
of upland heath and pricked occasionally by little rooftops. It is a very
beautiful sight. But not the end!

Walk back to the car along the ridge top path, a quicker and easier way
than the outward route, and eventually drop down to Bonehill Rocks, a tor
more complex than most and standing high above its surrounding sward. The
way to the top is around the back: into a broad 'chimney' between two large
slabs and then up the right-hand side. If it is for you then the ascent makes a
fitting end to a good walk. Now Widecombe's cafes are justly famous!

15. Crow Tor & the Beardown Tors

Start and finish: SX 609750
Distance: 9km (5¹/₂ miles)
Approximate time: 3 hours

There are not many compulsory walks on Dartmoor, but in part this is one! Not because of scenery or height, but to visit Wistman's Wood. The wood is popular: it combines a valley, running water, 'overhanging' tors and, of course, the little wood itself, all within walking distance of a car park and a busy pub. The car park, in a quarry opposite the Two Bridges Hotel, is a starting point for walks into the northern moor and is invariably full at weekends with cars and school minibuses. The hotel is an attractive building in a lovely vale and always busy, especially at Sunday lunchtimes. It is busy even on autumn days, when the morning has shrouded the hills around Princetown in a dense blanket of fog so that vehicles move slowly with their headlights burning indistinctly; their drivers unconscious of the blue sky and bright sunshine which is spreading warmth across the rest of Devon. Dartmoor is of modest height, but even so the weather changes very quickly. The visitor driving from Tavistock to Princetown early on an autumn morning can move from sunshine to mist and back to sunshine in the twinkling of an eye, all sheltered by the car: but the walker, faced with the same changes, experiences them more slowly and must be prepared to change clothes in order to conserve body heat, or to stay cool.

A track heads north from the car park to Crockern Cottage, with Crockern Tor on the hill to the right. The tor is the historic site of the meeting place of the Stannary Parliament which assembled to enact legislation for Dartmoor's tin miners. Below, and to the left, is the West Dart River, and on the far bank Beardown Hill rises steeply under its dark green swathe of pine trees. Beyond the cottage the track deteriorates to become a moorland footpath, staying well above the river and crossing successive drystone walls. (This is not really a dog walk, unless you are both adept at crossing stiles.) Otherwise it is easy going, level and dry underfoot, with a clear path following the valley northwards into the moor. Two kilometres ahead, standing slightly above the meanders of the West Dart River, is the distinctive block of Crow Tor, and to your left is the wider spread of rock on the Beardown Tors with the level line of the Devonport Leat sketched across its base. The footpath heads onwards along the western flank of Longaford Tor, a good crag which lies like an inverted yacht's keel along the ridge of high ground to your right, and leads eventually to the southern tip of Wistman's Wood.

The wood is one of a handful of ancient stands of dwarf oak which cling to steep and rocky valleys on the flanks of Dartmoor, and it is of easier access

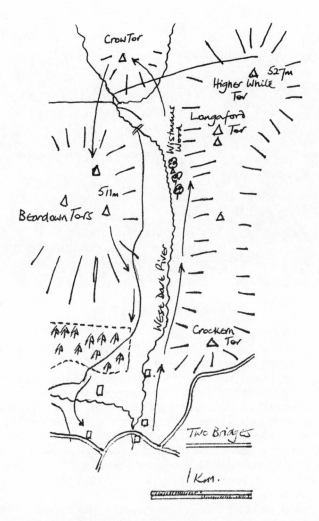

than the others. The little wood is undeniably mysterious: it is unexpected; it is old; it is all but impenetrable; and it is dwarf and hung about with mosses and lichen. So the sight of crimson rowan berries on the northern edge of the wood is a bright and cheerful flash of colour, all the more welcome as the last of the mist burns off to reveal a warm autumn day and the moorland rising on every hand in gentle golden curves towards an empty blue sky.

Beyond the wood the path splits: the left fork heads down to the weir at the head of the Devonport Leat, but your path heads upwards and towards Crow Tor. Follow the path as it becomes uncertain in places, and occasionally wet underfoot (this *is* Dartmoor!), rising over a gentle crest of grass and

The interior of Wistman's Wood.

Karen Lang

bracken and then losing itself amongst the tussocks and sheep trails. As the path fades away, so you will see the West Dart River swing across your front, following a line parallel with a drystone wall beyond. The wall is marked with three stiles, and the distinctive rock of Crow Tor rises above.

Drop down to the river, finding your own way through the heather, cross and then ascend to a stile, before climbing finally to reach Crow Tor itself. You are right on the edge of the range areas here, with red and white boundary poles intermittently marking the land, and empty flagpoles on the hilltops. Clamber to the top and enjoy the view back down the valley. You are not high enough to look into the northern moor, but you are in a position to enjoy a gentle moorland valley with rocks and water all around.

Here, where the valleys are deep and the land is bony, the tinners came to scratch the surface of the earth for minerals. The foundations of abandoned huts are their sole memorial.

Just below Crow Tor, to the south, is an area marked on the map as 'Foxholes'. Two watercourses meet nearby, three or four walls cross in the valley bottom and half a dozen tors rise above. It can be a tricky little bit of navigation to get through here with dry feet, so after scrambling around Crow Tor head downhill with care, aiming for the steeply-rising ground beyond and then the Beardown Tors above. There are no paths, except where the walls and streams force walkers into narrow gaps, but it is good exercise as you pull up the 70 or 80m from the valley bottom to the 513m hilltop beyond! From there

Crow Tor.
Karen Lang

you can see the silver thread of the Devonport Leat running southwards back towards Two Bridges. Drop down towards the leat, even though it is uncomfortable going diagonally across steeply-sloping and untracked ground, and then cross over the water to follow the path on the eastern side. Leat walking is one of Dartmoor's unique pleasures: invariably level, following the contours of the land in wide curves, and beside an abundant stream of fast-running clear water offering the occasional glimpse of a lithe and cautious trout. This leat leads into Beardown Wood: its cool and scented pines winding close around the water and the path, and shutting out Dartmoor's wide horizons.

The path brings you out at Beardown Farm, with a choice of routes back to Two Bridges, where a wide range of refreshments awaits you.

Winter

16. **Sittaford Tor**

17. **Hangingstone Hill**

18. **Penn Beacon & Shell Top**

19. **Mel Tor, Hockinston Tor & Leigh Tor**

20. **Cosdon Beacon**

Leigh Tor

G Thurlow

——————— 16. Sittaford Tor ———————

Start and finish: SX 669839
Distance: 9km (5¹/₂ miles)
Approximate time: 2 hours

The reservoirs provide some of Dartmoor's most magnetic landscapes, and on the whole they are carefully managed: car parks are discrete and there is no commercialisation beyond the occasional ice cream van. Their attraction is a casual by-product of urban exploitation, each lake serving the needs of one or more of the towns and cities on the edge of the moor. Today, whilst the artifical lakes continue to provide drinking water, they also serve to delight the eye and to provide a source of pleasure for visitors during every season of the year. Fernworthy, on the eastern side of the moor, lies within the embrace of a pine forest, a gracious stand of tall trees that comes almost to the water's edge on the lake's western shoreline.

Despite its innate beauty, Fernworthy is not particularly easy of access. The local roads are narrow, twisting around small fields, now climbing and then dropping down to little bridges or the occasional ford. On a winter morning, under a brilliant sun and cloudless sky, these roads will be treacherous with ice on the steeper climbs untouched by the day's scant warmth, and car tyres will spin as drivers feel their way cautiously through the countryside. From the west the lake is approached through Postbridge and then the tiny hamlets of Jurston and Corndon: from the east through Moretonhampstead, and from the north through Chagford. It's not far from the main road across the moor, and at busy times of the day the driver must be patient, stopping and pausing, reversing and waving, in order to allow the steady flow of two-way vehicle traffic along roads designed for a solitary tractor.

In this winter landscape the forest stands in dark contrast to the faded yellow of the surrounding moorland grasses. The green is intense, its colour drawn from the close-packed trees and tight-meshed branches, and then painted across the skyline without variation of shade. The road ahead glitters in the sunshine reflected off the melting ice.

The lake is visible through the trees around the deserted car park, a smiling Mediterranean blue in contrast to golden slopes on the far northern shore. The air smells cold, catching at the nostrils, and is scented with peat, pine and granite. (I swear that you can smell the rock on the high moor!)

The destination of this walk is Sittaford Tor, lying to the west of Fernworthy at a height of 538m, and on the edge of the heart of the northern moor. The route takes us from the car park, on foot, along the metalled road through the forest, and passing the southern shore of the lake.

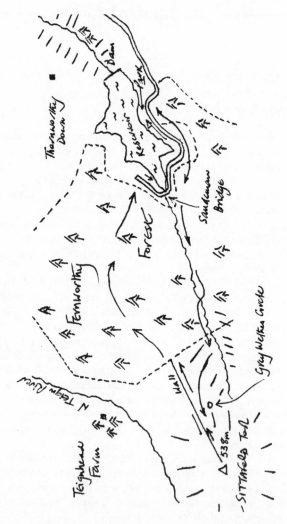

The dark trees stand erect and tall along each side of the road; on the left a wall of silence and shadow lies between you and the low-lying winter sun. On the road, in the dark canyon cut through the timber, it is bitterly cold and the tarmac is still skimmed with a thin layer of ice. A breeze cuts through fleece, wool and cotton, and in the shadow of the timber it is time to don windproofs.

The road faithfully follows the erratic outline of the lakeside, with little regard for slopes – up and down. Follow it, walking swiftly to keep warm, and pausing only to watch a heron's leisurely ascent from a pool in the stream flowing down to the lake, until you reach Sandeman Bridge. Down there the trees are further apart, and sunlight splashes gold and green across their highest branches in vivid contrast to the darkness beneath. To the right the lake sparkles, and overhead the sky is blue. This is cold front weather at its most stimulating, even if it is an effort to keep warm! Turn into the woods immediately beyond the bridge, heading west to the sharply-delineated boundary between forest and heath, and conscious that route-finding in woodland, where the foresters create new routes and old ones blocked by storm damage quickly become overgrown, can be an exercise in guesswork!

The wide footpath through the forest climbs gently upwards with the valley of a small stream to the right, at one point descending briefly to cross the water, before lifting again up to the final edge of the trees. Here the path emerges alongside the stream, which is flowing back into the trees and on down to the lake. Ascend the bare northern bank of the stream, looking back to glimpse the lake gleaming blue between the treetops below, and then push on until the stone circles of Grey Wethers are in sight. Wethers are sheep, and the story has it that these rocks have been sold as such on foggy days! The walking is fairly easy and level: in winter there may be a dusting of snow, with each blade of grass burdened by the weight of its heavy granular lining of white. Where it is wet the pools of peaty water may be greasy with a slick coat of melting ice, but out in the sunshine on these uplands the wind, once so merciless in the forest's gloomy shade, is now a tonic.

The stone circles of Grey Wethers, below Sittaford Tor.

Karen Lang

Sittaford Tor sits directly above the stones, a short green path through the golden heath connecting the two. From the summit the view is largely to the south and north, an inner moorland view to be relished patiently with the aid of map and compass. In the northern shadow behind the tor, frost and the dusting of snow will linger late into the winter's day, but for now your guide is the arrowstraight drystone wall heading north-east back to the forest. Walk downhill alongside the wall to a gate in the perimeter fence and then follow the forest paths, with their alpine lining of snow on the verges and the scent of pine, until they lead you to the road, just above Sandeman Bridge.

A little further on take the waymarked footpath along the water's edge, and linger amongst the sights, sounds and scents of Fernworthy as you make your way back to the car.

——————— 17. Hangingstone Hill ———————

Start and finish: SX 605897
Distance: 10km (6¹/4 miles)
Approximate time: 3 hours

The view northwards from the military ring road, near O.P. 15.

Karen Lang

From the centre of Okehampton take the road south to Okehampton Camp, signposted in the scarlet military style. The road heads uphill, gently at first, past suburban Edwardian villas and the junction with Station Road. It then becomes increasingly steep until it rears up, over the railway line and over the A30, higher still and higher, over the edge of the moor before suddenly stopping at the perimeter of the army camp, situated on the northern edge of the Okehampton military range.

Skirting the camp, with its barracks and security fence, a narrow road continues across a little granite bridge, and then heads off right into the centre of the northern moor. This road is one of Devon's best-kept secrets! The truth is that it is quite possible to drive into this marvellous wilderness. You can picnic alongside the road and enjoy some of England's most spectacular upland views without stepping from your camper van. And all of this because the range is maintained from a circular road, largely, but not wholly, metalled, which runs from Okehampton Camp around the whole inner sanctum of the northern moor and then back to the camp again. Follow the road south and east, past East Okement Farm, taking care when the metal breaks down to granite and gravel, until you reach the first serious ford: well it is a military road and was not designed for sports cars!

Park somewhere convenient and step out up the hill, following the quiet road southwards. The smooth dark moorland stretches out on either hand, held in the cold embrace of a low sun and the penetrating November breeze. You may

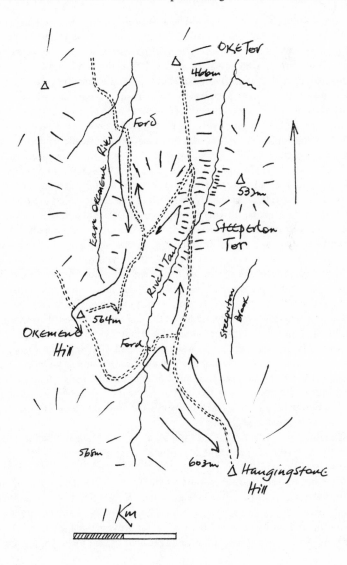

be passed by the occasional car as you pace evenly uphill, heading for the first crest a few hundred metres above the ford, but otherwise there is silence. It is worth pausing there to look back and around, as the spot provides a panorama extending from Wild Tor in the east, through Steeperton and the northern edge of the moor, and then out to the west to High Willhays. In the centre are the woods around East Okement, and beyond them lies the upper scarp of the moor, near the military camp, and then the hazy lowlands spread out into north Devon.

Turn your back on all of this and head steadily on upwards, trending to the right towards Okement Hill. To your left is the valley of the young River Taw and to your right the shallower valley of the East Okement. From the ford where you started, which was at about 410m, the road climbs 150m to Okement Hill with its massive observation post, the junction of three roads and a magnificent 360° panorama. Over it all towers the overwhelming Dartmoor skyscape: on a winter afternoon composed of low golden sunlight, filtered through bars of grey-white cloud and set in a bone blue sky. The wind plucks at your coat and you search for your gloves. To the south-east, and looking closer than it really is, lies your destination – Hangingstone Hill.

The metalled road breaks down to a granite track, brown, white and clean-looking, as it takes a level route across the top of the hill, south and east. On each side of the ridge rise the rivers of north Dartmoor – flowing north the Taw and the Okements, flowing south the East Dart and Teign: stray off the track and it's guaranteed to be wet underfoot. The once smooth track starts to descend, rougher underfoot, swinging to the left and giving up hard-won height to drop down to another small ford, this time across the headwaters of the Taw. Reluctantly you glance up to the right towards Hangingstone Hill, and your eye catches a snipe lifting silently from the rough grass, startled by your presence. Soon, though, you start to rise once more, to where the track ends and breaks down to a simple footpath. You are still lower than Okement Hill, but the objective is in sight again, due south.

Gradually the narrow footpath steepens, and Hangingstone disappears behind the first horizon. You pick a way through stones and peat until, suddenly, the observation post and the cairn are there. This is a 600m hilltop, a true high point and right at the very heart of the moor. This is Dartmoor! There is Fernworthy Forest, and there is Fur Tor. And, if you look to the south-east, is that flat line the Channel?

Hangingstone Hill was named for a logan stone, long ago. The huge rock, naturally pivoted and responsive to a fingertip, is, like most of its kind, long since grounded.

Time has moved on. An hour and a half behind you is the car and up here the sun is dropping close to the horizon, its level light flooding the landscape from underneath the low western clouds. Huge towers of cumulus glow gold and red, their cold light etched out by bars of grey and deeper black. As the year runs its course every walk has to be planned against the daylight, and the

Looking back towards Oke Tor (left) and Steeperton Tor.

Karen Lang

sensible walker watches the time remaining as his day on the hill progresses. It is time to leave.

The descent follows the path north, dropping quickly down to rejoin the track. From the junction continue north into the Taw Valley, down to the river under Steeperton Tor, to cross just above Steeperton Gorge. The footpath is a little tenuous in places as it drops slowly down above the meandering watercourse in the increasingly steep-sided ravine. Cross the water beyond the abandoned mine workings, head up the other side and turn briefly south-west, before rejoining the original road and then your car.

Drive slowly home in the gathering shadows and, after passing the camp, hang briefly above the evening lights of Okehampton in the darkness below the moor's northern edge. Then plunge back down the road into town and continue home past Okehampton Castle's gothic splendour. Time for a beer?

———— 18. Penn Beacon & Shell Top ————

Start and finish: SX 606615
Distance: 5km (3 miles)
Approximate time: 1¹/2 hours

North of the A38 the moor and the old Devonshire countryside blend into one another. This is the warm and sheltered side of the moor, where narrow lanes, overhung by trees, tangle like a blackthorn hedge, and crawl slowly around little fields, their edges green with moss. In places such as Cadover Bridge, with its ice cream vans and ample parking, access to the moor is easy, but for this walk the moor lies at the end of narrow roads and narrower tracks, which are cut by flood water courses after heavy rain. But at the end of such tracks, through the moor gates, beyond the last drystone wall, and where the bridle paths break down into worn peat gullies, there is the moor – silent and rising steeply upwards into the wind-clean blue winter sky.

When the country has been gripped by a hard frost and the land lies white under a cold yellow sun, the moorland walker drives carefully to his destination over unsalted roads, and slowly into the blinding low light of an early eastern sky. This is a mild place, where the east-facing slopes of pasture quickly show vivid emerald against the surrounding fields of frost, and in the distance perspectives of low white cloud give the impression of immense snowfields rising smoothly up towards some distant, but as yet invisible, summit. The overwhelming temptation is to leave home without the encumbrance of maps, compasses and layers of clothing: the sky is blue and the sun is not only bright but feels warm on the garage door. Do not be tempted ...

For this walk drive towards Cornwood, taking care in the early morning on the yet icy road. From the crossroads in the centre of the village head slowly towards the 'rookery', turning left at Rook Lane End and up Rook Lane (all the placenames between here and the moor seem to relate to rooks), and then find somewhere to park near East Rook Gate. This is not a tourist honeypot. This is not a visitor's right of way. Do not impede field gates, and do leave room for tractors! There is not much space; it may at most be enough for three cars if your predecessors have been thoughtful in their own parking. If, however, it is full, then change your plans for the day – the moor won't mind.

The walker should head north up the narrow water-rutted track, passing fields and occasional trees on either hand. To your right, about half a mile away, is the River Yealm, its wooded slopes out of sight and 180m or more below the river's rising at Yealm Head, two and a half miles upstream. Step through East Rook Gate at 260m and tramp directly ahead uphill, making your own path over the frost-hardened ground. Your destinations, Penn Beacon (427m) and

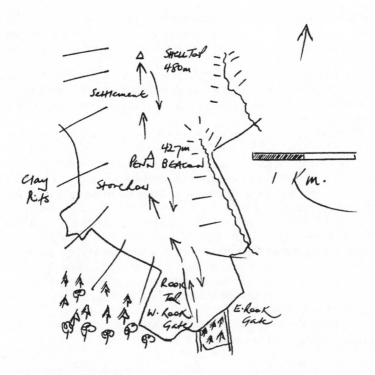

Shell Top (493m), are hidden by the intervening ground, and to your left Rook Tor is barely worth the diversion as Penn Beacon finally comes into sight. There are a couple of leats to cross, and the walking is easy with the sun on your back. But this is mid-winter and the wind is from the north: gloves, balaclava and hat are all essential, as with every knot of wind the relative temperature drops even further. And, although you may soon feel hot inside your windproofs, the exposed skin of your nose and lips will tell a different story!

The ground is crunchy underfoot, the grass brittle in the shadows where frost persists and the soil everywhere has a thin frozen crust. Pools of standing water glitter, the thin ice reflecting the cold bright sunshine. The beacon, as its name foretells, is another of the moor's good viewing points. At this time of year, with a low winter sun in the southern sky, the distant landscape is misty and your steady gaze will earn a windblown tear or two from watering eyes! But suddenly, and almost under your feet, your attention is drawn towards the vast clay workings, where acres of the moor's edge have been resculptured by massive spoil heaps and deep pits. To urban eyes it seems a terrible contradiction to the wildness of the moor, but in truth these workings are but an extension of the quarrying and mineral extraction that has been part of the

Dartmoor ecology for millennia – although not previously on quite this scale! And, as if to remind us of historical continuity in this landscape, the map records large areas of ancient settlements, cairns and boundary works on the lower slopes of the beacon.

Beyond Lee Moor lie Plymouth, the Sound and the Channel: the Channel is like a magnet to the eyes from a hundred viewpoints across the southern edge of Dartmoor, its distant gleam a reminder of the world beyond the South West Approaches.

The track beckons due north, its darker green running like an arrow towards Shell Top; and our long winter shadow lies flat across the Earth, pointing the way ahead. It is an easy, long-paced stroll up the gentle rise towards this peak – our final objective for the morning – and it consists of a small granite tor with someone's initials cut deeply into the flat top. On this day the wind is sharp and cold: each tussock of grass casts a shadow on the flat ground behind, leaving a dark microclimate where white frosts persist over areas little larger than a handspan. There is no view to the north-east, where the moor extends deeper inland, but on every other side the view opens out, across Cornwall, to the sea and then to the south-east as well. But in this light and this wind it is a landscape drained of colour, where blacks, whites and greys blur away the detail of woodland, field and village. It is too cold to linger and time to head back.

In summer the walk can easily be extended over Trowlesworthy and to Cadover, but today head south and back to the car!

Shell Top.
Karen Lang

—— 19. Mel Tor, Hockinston Tor & Leigh Tor ——

Start and finish: SX 695731
Distance: 8km (5 miles)
Approximate time: 2 hours

In the valleys and on the slopes surrounding high ground such as Dartmoor, the climate is more extreme: frosts are harder in the valley bottoms and mist lingers longer in the haggard woodlands. The unfolding landscape also unveils variety in the weather, and canny locals can dodge the worst on one side of the hills to find better on another, whilst the ignorant holiday visitor too often leaves for home with a single clammy memory of steady rain and damp waterproofs at the camp site.

Facing into the moist south-west airstreams, Dartmoor's western slopes breast the cloud around the tors, where mist magnifies the shattered shapes of the rocky peaks and distorts perspective. However, in the lee of the moor, 20 miles to the east, the same mist rapidly burns off, to show the swelling sunlit curves of distant countryside falling away in folds of shadow towards Exeter.

In settled periods of cold weather, when Devon is at peace under an area of high pressure, banks of fog can lie on the edge of the moor, sloping up into the empty blue sky like unshadowed alpine snowfields, but even then there is often a contrast between the west and the east; one is frequently grey whilst the other is sun bright. The best weather of all is after a snowfall onto hard ground with no prospect of a thaw – these are the Dartmoor dog days. Then, and on a Sunday early after the church bells, the eastern upland will be empty of traffic and people, and the only sound will be the high and distant rumble of passenger aircraft ribboning westward, white and silver, Atlantic-bound.

On the south-east of the moor the river valleys cut back deep from the South Hams into the treeless peat watersheds. Narrow roads and rushing streams descend abruptly under dark trees which steeple the dark slopes under the rocky tors.

Of these rivers, the Dart is seen at its wildest from a position just below Bel Tor, in itself a popular viewpoint and car stop, but best left quickly behind by heading off towards Mel Tor and scrambling up to its little top. Nearly 120m below you is the Dart Gorge, a narrow ribbon of water between the trees. After rain, and if it is quiet, you may be able to hear the river's voice. Opposite you is Venford Reservoir and nearer is Bench Tor, squat and low viewed from here and hiding its steep and rugged eastern faces. This lovely view captures some of the best of Dartmoor: a small landscape but complex – in literary terms a Jane Austen when compared to the Tolstoyan Alps: a very English charm.

The bridlepath behind Mel Tor is Doctor Blackall's Drive, constructed in

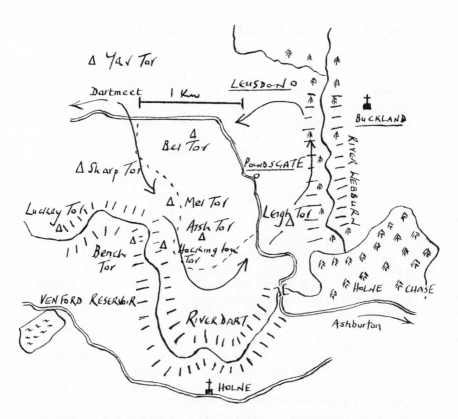

the 19th century to enable the owner of Spitchwick Manor to absorb the view from his carriage. We, of course, enjoy it on foot, following his path south-eastwards, past Hockinston Tor (below, on the right, and worth a diversion for the view) towards Aish Tor, but ruing the gentle downward slope where every step means a more painful upward climb later. In the meantime, thank the good doctor for this view!

Follow the drive until you reach the road, cross it and pick up the short track down to Leigh Tor. Like so many of Dartmoor's lesser crags, Leigh Tor reveals little of its interest from the path. Here, as elsewhere on the eastern side of the moor, the rocks poke out from the hillside and the hill climbs away above the rocks, so that the tor seems insignificant when approached from above; little more than another jumble of boulders. Pick your way down past the trees and saplings to the right of the rocks, staying close to the base. After descending a few metres stop, look up to the skyline, and touch the rock. This is schorl, a mixture of tourmaline and granite, which gives Leigh Tor its character of edges, cubes and angles. Elsewhere, Dartmoor's tors are almost invariably of granite, piled slabs of rock, smoothed with almost feminine

Part of the rock face of Leigh Tor.
Author

curves by the weather, but here is a tor with fault lines and angular holds which offers easy scrambling for the adventurous, and another of Dartmoor's lovely valley views. The inexperienced can reach the top without difficulty from the other side of the tor, picking a route between the slabs of stone to a little saddle on the crest. On a quiet day this is the place to open your flask of tea and wait for the buzzards to circle the woodland below.

The route back to your car is largely uphill and through more domestic scenery. Dropping down to the valley, and staying on this side of the river, follow your nose left alongside the River Dart as it tumbles downstream. Before the confluence with the River Webburn strike off northwards towards Leusdon, through Spitchwick. The rights of way and access in this corner of the national park are a tangle and further confused by the presence of two rivers apparently flowing in opposite directions, so you will definitely need a map to make sense of the roads and pathways. There is a pleasing English variety of scenery on a miniature scale: contrasting overshadowed deciduous woods with steep root-twined footpaths and neatly-swarded parkland with metalled roads, all following the Two Moors Way past the pretty church of St John the Baptist, with its attractive Arts and Crafts stained glass, and on to Ponsworthy. From there head back to Bel Tor along the footpath from Sweaton.

This is a walk of halves: the first downhill on the moor, the second largely uphill in its verdant and mossy valleys. Uniting the two was the real aim of the walk – Leigh Tor, where I do hope you managed to scramble up its steeper side before looking out towards Deeper Marsh and Holne Chase.

20. Cosdon Beacon

Start and finish: SX 620935
Distance: 6km (3³/4 miles)
Approximate time: 3 hours

The starting point of this walk to the top of Cosdon Beacon is Belstone, a moorland village where small Edwardian villas mingle with much older cottages and houses, all built of the austere grey granite that you also find in small Scottish seaside towns. But this is an upland place where cold rain beats down the autumnal chimney smoke, and where, in summer, the rising ground spills scents of heather, peat and rock into the little streets. In the 1970s this area was also the location for one of those gems of a film which we make from time to time in this country, called 'The Belstone Fox'. I hope that you have had the good fortune to see it.

There is space to park a few cars on the verge beside the road, just beyond the good little pub and the small church, St Mary's, which clings to the side of the hill for shelter. At the bottom of the narrow valley, 30m below the cars and overlooked by the last houses in the village, the Taw tumbles off the moor and turns sharply east into the wooded gap of Belstone Cleave: beyond there the river flows out into lower lands and then runs steadily north to the Bristol Channel. From here, and looking to the other side of the river, the land rears up steeply back into the moor through gorse and birch, sweeping past a stone wall on the slope above the cleave and on to meet a swelling horizon of moorland grass and heather. With luck, you may spot the bridlepath opposite if a walker is coming down past the wall and through the patchy gorse. That is where you are going. It is a tough little route: you need a map, boots and a compass, but the reward is a spectacular view, especially on a clear winter day. The drawback is a river crossing on the way back and, oh yes, it can be a bit of a plod!

From your car drop quickly down across the turf past the picnickers towards the river, and near the bottom pick up a steep and stony path which, after rain, looks and feels more like an ambitious infant stream bed. The map shows the footbridge over the Taw lying just beyond the path. The bridge itself is a handsome little timber structure and it has a gate at each end with muddy, well-worn approaches. It is also the first bridge over the Taw, and for some kilometres above Belstone the river is not so easily crossed.

On the other side your path ascends to the right through the scrub, and then continues to rise steadily before following the contours eastward across the lifting moorland. To the right of your path the windswept grass rises in a swelling curve to Cosdon Beacon, which is still invisible beyond the close, but bare, horizon. Behind you, and to the west, the little pinnacles of Belstone Tor

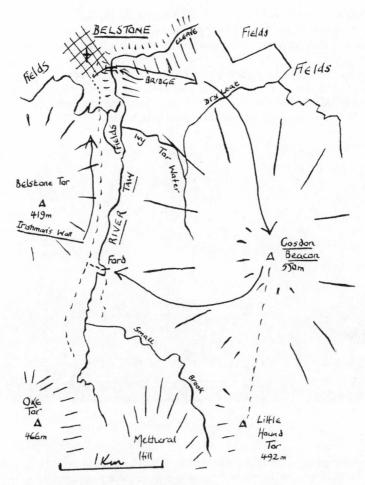

and Common still seem to be slightly higher.

Above here the moor drains across the path and down into the Taw, but the bridlepath picks a dry-shod route between the sodden stands of tussocky peat until, at a height of about 350m and above Belstone Cleave, the surrounding ground gradually dries out. Here your route turns south, off the bridlepath and directly up over the grass and heather towards the top, which is about a kilometre and a half away. Turn right and head for the highest point in sight.

In December you will, with luck and planning, be under a low sun below a cold blue sky chased with silver-grey cloud. Underfoot, the coarse grass plucks at your bootlaces, and the rough tussocks guide your feet into little sheep-nibbled paths that wander haphazardly across the slope. Cross the narrow dry leat and then, higher up, you will reach a square of vegetation which has been fenced off from stock: within it, thickly and well grown, is a patch of vigorous colours in a steppe otherwise composed from a pale winter palette. From the fence you can pick out the cairns which crown the beacon above you, puncturing the otherwise fetureless curve across the topmost horizon. Stop and look back. The view to the north has opened with your height, and deepened into the sunlit winter countryside below. Dappled by slow flotillas of cloud shadow, and chequered by hedge boundaries, the lovely landscape fades slowly into the distant northern haze.

The old trig point on the summit of Cosdon.

Karen Lang

Press on to the first cairn and then the few extra yards to the old trig point close by. Step onto the highest stone and from there you command a 360° panorama. First look south-westwards across the eastern flanks of Dartmoor. More than 15km away, on the far side of the moor, you will see the distinctive shape of Hay Tor, with Hound Tor in front, just above Widecombe and not far from Ashburton. The real reason for the walk, however, is the view that extends from in front of you (south) westwards around the horizon to High Willhays and Yes Tor on your furthest right. This empty expanse embraces a vast and shallow amphitheatre almost 6km across and nearly 10km deep, sloping slightly northwards and containing the headwaters of the Taw and the East Okement. On a late winter morning the low sunlight throws long shadows across a dead brown land, picking out the dark upthrust rocks of Steeperton Tor and Hangingstone Hill and drawing brushstrokes of faded gold onto the gentler slopes of Oke Tor. Directly opposite, and across the Taw, the little scree field on the eastern slope of Belstone Tor is the closest that this once frost-shattered landscape approaches alpine scenery. The grey scatter of rocks look like stark ribs in a winter carcase.

The perimeter of Dartmoor is blessed with a handful of excellent high viewpoints, but Cosdon Beacon is amongst the very best. From here you can look into the heart of the northern moor, and at other seasons, if you are lucky, you will put up a curlew, grouse or lapwing, or watch a buzzard circling over the lower slopes. If you wish, there is a well-worn track heading south. It would be easy going at first and runs towards Postbridge, but our walk heads, instead, to a ford below Higher Tor. As you look at Belstone Tor there is a drystone wall known as 'Irishman's Wall' to the left of the scree. The ford through the Taw, which is your next objective, is to the left of the wall, but the low-lying ground between the foot of Cosdon Beacon and the river is marshy. Aim a hand's breadth to the left of the wall, and set off down the hill. There is some clitter and a small fragment of rock on the way down. From there you will see a low shelf of slightly higher land which skirts the left of the marshy ground ahead. Follow the lip of this shelf towards the river, still heading to the left of Irishman's Wall, and you will, in due course, reach the ford which lies at a distinctive meander. If the weather has been very dry, and if your boots are good, it may be possible to cross the river here without getting your feet wet. Otherwise do as I did: paddle over and carry your boots and stockings. It is harmless and stimulating! Dry your feet on your stocking tops.

The path north goes directly back to Belstone and your car. It takes you through a typical Dartmoor scene (the junction between the moor and enclosed land) – stone walls and worn granite stones bedded in the cattle-worn earth, overhung by small trees, and with rugged moorland separated from a rough wall-contained track by an old wooden gate. Beyond is a mix of cottages and upland barns, somewhat gentrified but still preserving the true character of upland villages. Cold air, thick-walled houses, rough granite and the tantalising scent of woodsmoke make sure of that.

A bit of a plod? Not really!

———————— The Gazetteer ————————

The two lists that follow are based on names and spellings on the Landranger Ordnance Survey Map 1:25,000. They contain the peaks within the bounds of Dartmoor which have the title 'tor' on that map, and all other significant hilltops. Some may complain at the omission of tors whose names appear on smaller scale maps; others may dispute the exclusion of a favourite hilltop as 'insignificant'. However, any interesting list will be partisan to an extent and so, to inform the new visitor as well as to provide some 'colour', the lists also grade the peaks with a star category which ranges from one star (*) to four (****).

This star system is based on personal assessment, drawing for inspiration on such factors as a peak's height, the view which it commands, the shape of the rock, its merit as a scramble, or even half-forgotten memories of a particularly good walk in! Inevitably such valuations will attract disagreement and criticism, and any reader is welcome to amend the pages to reflect their personal views, but a visitor new to the moor, or new to an area of the moor, should find this gazetteer both a stimulation and an entertainment, as a geographical catalogue of hilltops graded by height and quality.

Note: The height given (in metres) is either the adjacent spot height on the map or an interpolation by the author. Six-figure grid references (prefixed SX on Dartmoor) are used as an aid to location.

1. Alphabetical List

	Name	Grid Ref.	Height	Stars	Date Visited
1	Aish Tor	704715	283	*	
2	Arch Tor	635782	410	*	
3	Arms Tor	541863	457	**	
4	Bag Tor	762775	349	*	
5	Baggator	548805	372	**	
6	Beardown Tors	603775	513	**	
7	Bel Tor	695729	354	*	
8	Bell Tor	731778	400	*	
9	Bellever Tor	645765	443	**	
10	Belstone Tor	615924	479	***	
11	Bench Tor	692718	312	***	
12	Birch Tor	686816	487	***	
13	Black Hill	762787	412	*	

	Name	Grid Ref.	Height	Stars	Date Visited
14	Black Tor	566895	488	**	
15	Black Tor	573717	350	*	
16	Black Tor	678636	320	**	
17	Blackadon Tor	712734	280	***	
18	Blackingstone Rock	786856	335	***	
19	Bonehill Rocks	732775	393	**	
20	Boulters Tor	525782	336	***	
21	Bowerman's Nose	742805	390	***	
22	Bracken Tor	588938	290	*	
23	Branscombe's Loaf	554892	537	**	
24	Brat Tor	539856	452	***	
25	Brimhill Tor	518795	220	*	
26	Butterdon Hill	656586	362	***	
27	Calveslake Tor	607676	400	*	
28	Chat Tor	555852	542	*	
29	Chinkwell Tor	728781	400	***	
30	Combeshead Tor	588688	371	*	
31	Combestone Tor	670718	356	**	
32	Conies Down Tor	589791	525	*	
33	Coombe Tor	687871	259	*	
34	Corndon Tor	688743	434	**	
35	Cosdon Beacon	635915	550	****	
36	Cox Tor	531761	442	****	
37	Cramber Tor	583712	420	*	
38	Criptor	556727	313	*	
39	Crockern Tor	616757	400	**	
40	Crow Tor	607788	501	*	
41	Cut Hill	598828	603	**	
42	Devils Tor	597797	549	**	
43	Dewerstone, The	539639	227	****	
44	Dinger Tor	586881	550	**	
45	Doe Tor	542848	425	**	
46	Down Tor	581695	366	*	
47	Dunnagoat Tors	558864	550	*	
48	Easdon Tor	729823	439	***	
49	East Mill Tor 'A'	599901	487	**	
50	East Mill Tor 'B'	599897	513	**	
51	Eastern Tor	584665	333	*	
52	Eastern White Barrow	665652	474	***	
53	Feather Tor	535742	313	*	
54	Flat Tor	609815	540	*	
55	Foggin Tor	566736	401	*	

	Name	Grid Ref.	Height	Stars	Date Visited
56	Fox Tor	626698	438	*	
57	Fox Tor	515788	180	*	
58	Fur Tor	586831	573	****	
59	Ger Tor	546831	430	****	
60	Gidleigh Tor	673877	334	*	
61	Great Kneeset	589859	547	**	
62	Great Links Tor	552867	586	****	
63	Great Mis Tor	562768	538	***	
64	Great Nodden	539874	437	**	
65	Great Staple Tor	542760	455	****	
66	Great Trowlesworthy Tor	579644	357	***	
67	Greator Rocks	747787	371	****	
68	Green Tor	562865	546	*	
69	Gren Tor	551879	520	*	
70	Gutter Tor	577667	350	***	
71	Hameldown Beacon	708789	517	**	
72	Hameldown Tor	703806	529	**	
73	Hangingstone Hill	616861	603	****	
74	Hare Tor	551843	531	***	
75	Hart Tor	581720	390	*	
76	Hartland Tor	642799	410	**	
77	Hay Tor	757771	457	****	
78	Hawks Tor	553625	265	*	
79	Heckwood Tor	537738	320	*	
80	Heltor Rock	799871	310	***	
81	Hen Tor	594654	414	***	
82	High Tor	513787	180	*	
83	High Willhays	579895	621	****	
84	Higher Hartor Tor	602678	410	*	
85	Higher Tor	613917	480	*	
86	Higher White Tor	619785	527	***	
87	Hockinston Tor	696719	220	**	
88	Hollow Tor	731762	360	*	
89	Hollow Tor	571747	474	*	
90	Holwell Tor	752776	402	*	
91	Honeybag Tor	728787	445	***	
92	Hookney Tor	698814	497	***	
93	Hound Tor	628890	495	***	
94	Hound Tor	743790	414	***	
95	Huccaby Tor	657740	350	*	
96	Hucken Tor	549738	287	*	
97	Hunt Tor	556875	562	**	

	Name	Grid Ref.	Height	Stars	Date Visited
98	Hunters Tor	760824	326	***	
99	Hunters Tor	722897	240	*	
100	Ingra Tor	555721	339	*	
101	Kent's Tor	517794	220	*	
102	Kes Tor	666863	437	***	
103	King Tor	709815	488	**	
104	King's Tor	557738	400	***	
105	Kitty Tor	568875	570	**	
106	Laughter Tor	653758	420	***	
107	Leather Tor	563699	380	****	
108	Leedon Tor	564718	380	**	
109	Legis Tor	572655	310	**	
110	Leigh Tor	711715	180	***	
111	Lints Tor	579875	496	**	
112	Littaford Tor	615772	466	*	
113	Little Hound Tor	632898	492	*	
114	Little Links Tor	546869	510	**	
115	Little Mis Tor	565763	480	*	
116	Little Staple Tor	538754	380	*	
117	Little Trowlesworthy Tor	578646	340	**	
118	Longaford Tor	615780	507	***	
119	Longtimber Tor	509783	150	*	
120	Lower Hartor Tor	604678	390	**	
121	Lower White Tor	619793	507	*	
122	Luckey Tor	685720	200	***	
123	Lydford Tor	599781	501	*	
124	Lynch Tor	565806	517	**	
125	Manaton Rocks	748816	330	****	
126	Mel Tor	694725	346	***	
127	Meldon Hill	696861	390	**	
128	Middle Staple Tor	540755	431	*	
129	Middle Tor	669858	415	**	
130	Nat Tor	545824	350	*	
131	North Hessary Tor	578743	517	*	
132	Oke Tor	612901	466	***	
133	Okement Hill	602878	564	**	
134	Peek Hill	557699	400	**	
135	Penn Beacon	659629	427	**	
136	Pew Tor	532736	310	***	
137	Pil Tor	735759	420	*	
138	Pupers Hill	673674	467	***	
139	Ravens Tor	762819	250	*	

	Name	Grid Ref.	Height	Stars	Date Visited
140	Rippa Tor	643881	421	*	
141	Rippon Tor	747757	473	****	
142	Rook Tor	602617	295	*	
143	Roos Tor	543767	454	**	
144	Rough Tor	606798	547	**	
145	Row Tor	593917	468	**	
146	Rundlestone Tor	577746	490	*	
147	Ryder's Hill	659690	515	***	
148	Saddle Tor	751764	330	**	
149	Scarey Tor	606924	365	*	
150	Scorhill Tor	658872	370	*	
151	Shap Tor	808808	260	*	
152	Shapley Tor	698821	470	**	
153	Sharp Tor	550848	519	**	
154	Sharp Tor	687729	380	****	
155	Sharp Tor	649619	414	**	
156	Sharp Tor	728899	240	*	
157	Sharpitor	772815	262	***	
158	Sharpitor	559704	410	***	
159	Shavercombe Tor	594660	350	*	
160	Sheeps Tor	566683	369	****	
161	Shell Top	598638	470	***	
162	Shelstone Tor	559898	390	*	
163	Shilstone Tor	658902	314	*	
164	Shipley Tor	686632	300	*	
165	Sittaford Tor	634831	538	**	
166	Sourton Tors	542898	440	**	
167	South Hessary Tor	596724	450	**	
168	Standon Hill	555815	485	*	
169	Stannon Tor	646811	460	*	
170	Steeperton Tor	618887	540	***	
171	Steng-a-Tor	568880	540	*	
172	Tavy Cleave Tors	555834	440	***	
173	Ter Hill	643706	481	*	
174	Thornworthy Tor	665851	424	*	
175	Three Barrows	653626	461	****	
176	Top Tor	736764	432	*	
177	Ugborough Beacon	668592	378	****	
178	Vixen Tor	542742	380	****	
179	Watern Tor	628868	526	**	
180	Wels Tor	736730	380	****	
181	West Mill Tor	587909	541	***	

	Name	Grid Ref.	Height	Stars	Date Visited
182	Western Beacon	655575	334	***	
183	Western White Barrow	654654	481	*	
184	White Tor	543788	468	*	
185	Whitehorse Hill	617855	602	**	
186	Wild Tor	622876	531	**	
187	Wind Tor	708758	375	*	
188	Winter Tor	609916	420	*	
189	Yar Tor	678740	416	**	
190	Yes Tor	581902	619	****	

2. Height List

	Name	Grid Ref.	Height	Stars	Date Visited
1	High Willhays	579895	621	****	
2	Yes Tor	581902	619	****	
3	Cut Hill	598828	603	**	
4	Hangingstone Hill	616861	603	****	
5	Whitehorse Hill	617855	602	**	
6	Great Links Tor	552867	586	****	
7	Fur Tor	586831	573	****	
8	Kitty Tor	568875	570	**	
9	Okement Hill	602878	564	**	
10	Hunt Tor	556875	562	**	
11	Cosdon Beacon	635915	550	****	
12	Dinger Tor	586881	550	**	
13	Dunnagoat Tors	558864	550	*	
14	Devils Tor	597797	549	**	
15	Great Kneeset	589859	547	**	
16	Rough Tor	606798	547	**	
17	Green Tor	562865	546	*	
18	Chat Tor	555852	542	*	
19	West Mill Tor	587909	541	***	
20	Flat Tor	609815	540	*	
21	Steeperton Tor	618887	540	***	
22	Steng-a-Tor	568880	540	*	
23	Great Mis Tor	562768	538	***	
24	Sittaford Tor	634831	538	**	
25	Branscombe's Loaf	554892	537	**	
26	Hare Tor	551843	531	***	

	Name	Grid Ref.	Height	Stars	Date Visited
27	Wild Tor	622876	531	**	
28	Hameldown Tor	703806	529	**	
29	Higher White Tor	619785	527	***	
30	Watern Tor	628868	526	**	
31	Conies Down Tor	589791	525	*	
32	Gren Tor	551879	520	*	
33	Sharp Tor	550848	519	**	
34	Hameldown Beacon	708789	517	**	
35	Lynch Tor	565806	517	**	
36	North Hessary Tor	578743	517	*	
37	Ryder's Hill	659690	515	***	
38	Beardown Tors	603775	513	**	
39	East Mill Tor 'B'	599897	513	**	
40	Little Links Tor	546869	510	**	
41	Longaford Tor	615780	507	***	
42	Lower White Tor	619793	507	*	
43	Crow Tor	607788	501	*	
44	Lydford Tor	599781	501	*	
45	Hookney Tor	698814	497	***	
46	Lints Tor	579875	496	**	
47	Hound Tor	628890	495	***	
48	Little Hound Tor	632898	492	*	
49	Rundlestone Tor	577746	490	*	
50	Black Tor	566895	488	**	
51	King Tor	709815	488	**	
52	Birch Tor	686816	487	***	
53	East Mill Tor 'A'	599901	487	**	
54	Standon Hill	555815	485	*	
55	Ter Hill	643706	481	*	
56	Western White Barrow	654654	481	*	
57	Higher Tor	613917	480	*	
58	Little Mis Tor	565763	480	*	
59	Belstone Tor	615924	479	***	
60	Eastern White Barrow	665652	474	***	
61	Hollow Tor	571747	474	*	
62	Rippon Tor	747757	473	****	
63	Shapley Tor	698821	470	**	
64	Shell Top	598638	470	***	
65	Row Tor	593917	468	**	
66	White Tor	543788	468	*	
67	Pupers Hill	673674	467	***	
68	Littaford Tor	615772	466	*	

	Name	Grid Ref.	Height	Stars	Date Visited
69	Oke Tor	612901	466	***	
70	Three Barrows	653626	461	****	
71	Stannon Tor	646811	460	*	
72	Arms Tor	541863	457	**	
73	Hay Tor	757771	457	****	
74	Great Staple Tor	542760	455	****	
75	Roos Tor	543767	454	**	
76	Brat Tor	539856	452	***	
77	South Hessary Tor	596724	450	**	
78	Honeybag Tor	728787	445	***	
79	Bellever Tor	645765	443	**	
80	Cox Tor	531761	442	****	
81	Sourton Tors	542898	440	**	
82	Tavy Cleave Tors	555834	440	***	
83	Easdon Tor	729823	439	***	
84	Fox Tor	626698	438	*	
85	Great Nodden	539874	437	**	
86	Kes Tor	666863	437	***	
87	Corndon Tor	688743	434	**	
88	Top Tor	736764	432	*	
89	Middle Staple Tor	540755	431	*	
90	Ger Tor	546831	430	****	
91	Penn Beacon	659629	427	**	
92	Doe Tor	542848	425	**	
93	Thornworthy Tor	665851	424	*	
94	Rippa Tor	643881	421	*	
95	Cramber Tor	583712	420	*	
96	Laughter Tor	653758	420	***	
97	Pil Tor	735759	420	*	
98	Winter Tor	609916	420	*	
99	Yar Tor	678740	416	**	
100	Middle Tor	669858	415	**	
101	Hen Tor	594654	414	***	
102	Hound Tor	743790	414	***	
103	Sharp Tor	649619	414	**	
104	Black Hill	762787	412	*	
105	Arch Tor	635782	410	*	
106	Hartland Tor	642799	410	**	
107	Higher Hartor Tor	602678	410	*	
108	Sharpitor	559704	410	***	
109	Holwell Tor	752776	402	*	
110	Foggin Tor	566736	401	*	

	Name	Grid Ref.	Height	Stars	Date Visited
111	Bell Tor	731778	400	*	
112	Calveslake Tor	607676	400	*	
113	Chinkwell Tor	728781	400	***	
114	Crockern Tor	616757	400	**	
115	King's Tor	557738	400	***	
116	Peek Hill	557699	400	**	
117	Bonehill Rocks	732775	393	**	
118	Bowerman's Nose	742805	390	***	
119	Hart Tor	581720	390	*	
120	Lower Hartor Tor	604678	390	**	
121	Meldon Hill	696861	390	**	
122	Shelstone Tor	559898	390	*	
123	Leather Tor	563699	380	****	
124	Leeden Tor	564718	380	**	
125	Little Staple Tor	538754	380	*	
126	Sharp Tor	687729	380	****	
127	Vixen Tor	542742	380	****	
128	Wels Tor	736730	380	****	
129	Ugborough Beacon	668592	378	****	
130	Wind Tor	708758	375	*	
131	Baggator	548805	372	**	
132	Combeshead Tor	588688	371	*	
133	Greator Rocks	747787	371	****	
134	Scorhill Tor	658872	370	*	
135	Sheeps Tor	566683	369	****	
136	Down Tor	581695	366	*	
137	Scarey Tor	606924	365	*	
138	Butterdon Hill	656586	362	***	
139	Hollow Tor	731762	360	*	
140	Great Trowlesworthy Tor	579644	357	***	
141	Combestone Tor	670718	356	**	
142	Bel Tor	695729	354	*	
143	Black Tor	573717	350	*	
144	Gutter Tor	577667	350	***	
145	Huccaby Tor	657740	350	*	
146	Nat Tor	545824	350	*	
147	Shavercombe Tor	594660	350	*	
148	Bag Tor	762775	349	*	
149	Mel Tor	694725	346	***	
150	Little Trowlesworthy Tor	578646	340	**	
151	Ingra Tor	555721	339	*	
152	Boulters Tor	525782	336	***	

	Name	Grid Ref.	Height	Stars	Date Visited
153	Blackingstone Rock	786856	335	***	
154	Gidleigh Tor	673877	334	*	
155	Western Beacon	655575	334	***	
156	Eastern Tor	584665	333	*	
157	Manaton Rocks	748816	330	****	
158	Saddle Tor	751764	330	**	
159	Hunters Tor	760824	326	***	
160	Black Tor	678636	320	**	
161	Heckwood Tor	537738	320	*	
162	Shilstone Tor	658902	314	*	
163	Criptor	556727	313	*	
164	Feather Tor	535742	313	*	
165	Bench Tor	692718	312	***	
166	Heltor Rock	799871	310	***	
167	Legis Tor	572655	310	**	
168	Pew Tor	532736	310	***	
169	Shipley Tor	686632	300	*	
170	Rook Tor	602617	295	*	
171	Bracken Tor	588938	290	*	
172	Hucken Tor	549738	287	*	
173	Aish Tor	704715	283	*	
174	Blackadon Tor	712734	280	***	
175	Hawks Tor	553625	265	*	
176	Sharpitor	772815	262	***	
177	Shap Tor	808808	260	*	
178	Coombe Tor	687871	259	*	
179	Ravens Tor	762819	250	*	
180	Hunters Tor	722897	240	*	
181	Sharp Tor	728899	240	*	
182	Dewerstone, The	539639	227	****	
183	Brimhill Tor	518795	220	*	
184	Hockinston Tor	696719	220	**	
185	Kent's Tor	517794	220	*	
186	Luckey Tor	685720	200	***	
187	Fox Tor	515788	180	*	
188	High Tor	513787	180	*	
189	Leigh Tor	711715	180	***	
190	Longtimber Tor	509783	150	*	

Index